Alfred Jarry:
The Man with the Axe

D1557300

By the same author:
MARK TWAIN IN CALIFORNIA
THE SAGEBRUSH BOHEMIAN

By the same artist:
ZIPPY, NATION OF PINHEADS
ZIPPY STORIES
POINTED BEHAVIOR
ARE WE HAVING FUN YET?
PINDEMONIUM
KING PIN
PINHEAD'S PROGRESS
GET ME A TABLE WITHOUT FLIES, HARRY

ALFRED JARRY

THE MAN WITH THE AXE

by NIGEY LENNON with illustrations by BILL GRIFFITH

LAST GASP   San Francisco

DEDICATION

To Leslie Kamen, formerly of
Altadena but now a certifiable
New Yorker. L'amour et l'art.

Copyright © 1984 by Nigey Lennon

Illustrations copyright © 1984 by Bill Griffith

All rights reserved. No part of this book may be reprinted or reproduced in any form, except for brief excerpts which are part of a review, without permission in writing from the publisher.

First Last Gasp printing 1990

Library of Congress Cataloging in Publication Data

Lennon, Nigey, 1954-
    Alfred Jarry : the man with the axe.

    Bibliography: p.
    Includes index.
    1. Jarry, Alfred, 1873-1907. 2. Authors, French—
19th century—Biography. I. Title.
PQ2619.A65Z73   1984   842'.8 [B]   83-24312

ISBN 0-86719-382-4

Book design:
Bill Griffith

Computer typography and typesetting design:
Dianna Preston, Typesetter, at Freedmen's Organization, Los Angeles

Production and design coordination:
Nigey Lennon

The Epilogue ("Alfred Jarry—First Sublime Humorist of the Apocalypse") originally appeared in somewhat different form in *Arts and Architecture* magazine.

Last Gasp, Inc.
P.O. Box 410067
San Francisco, CA 94941

Previously published by Panjandrum Books.

Manufactured in the United States of America.

This book was funded in part by a grant from The National Endowment for the Arts, Literature Program, a federal agency.

Table of Contents

AUTHOR'S ACKNOWLEDGEMENTS

In the process of researching, writing, and producing this book, I received assistance, support, and inspiration from a number of people. If some of them are still fed up with me for being a persistent and seemingly oblivious nuisance, perhaps the thrill of seeing their names in print will reduce their annoyance. If not, I promise I'll never do it again—not until next time, anyway.

First, my thanks to my chief collaborator, Bill Griffith (the Satie of the Speedball), for his uncanny ability to transform my subconscious gropings into concrete images, improving and clarifying them considerably in the process; and for remaining steadfastly good-natured about everything (even the severe shrinkage in his prized postcard collection due to our voluminous correspondence);

to my husband Lionel Rolfe (author of those classic volumes, *Literary L.A.* and *The Menuhins: A Family Odyssey*), for his support, insights, free advice, 6 A.M. runs for double chili-cheeseburgers, and computer-related angst;

to John Ahouse, head of Special Collections at California State University, Long Beach, for his astute editing of the manuscript as well as for his invaluable research assistance;

to Dianna Preston, computer typesetter and typographer, for her unflagging enthusiasm, saintlike patience, eagle editing eye, and immediate grasp of the essence of pataphysics, especially regarding type design and layout;

to Dennis Koran, the Grand Panjandrum (and winner of the Young Henri Rousseau Lookalike Contest—prize: one vinyl Palmes Academiques medal), for moving his publishing empire from San Francisco to a location directly beneath the San Diego Freeway in Los Angeles, where he subsequently began publishing books on surrealism;

to Dr. Robert M. Rolfe and Messrs. Richard V. Wilson and Don Long, for all their time, sweat, and computer expertise during the agony of the data transfer process;

to Barbara Goldstein, publisher of *Arts and Architecture* magazine, for her belief in the project and for her generous sharing of resources; and to her husband John Pastier, for always laughing at my jokes;

to Ken Hense (the Mad Synthesist of Mar Vista), for tapes of his music, which created the perfect ambience for writing a book called *The Man with the Axe*—not to mention for being the inventor of the "Pinhead Punch" (Vandermint liqueur and tomato juice) imbibed by Jarry in *The Pataphysician*;

to Benjamin L. Rolfe, my father-in-law, for legal advice and other support;

to Tyler Owlglass, Ph.D. and Maestro Alfredo Fettuccini, dishonorable Regents of the Los Angeles Institute of Quantum 'Pataphysics, for less than I have room to list;

and finally, to Urban Gwerder of Zurich, pataphysical cowboy and independent publisher *par excellence*, for championing Jarry's dubious cause in so many different languages.

ARTIST'S ACKNOWLEDGEMENT

Bill Griffith would like to extend his thanks to Joyce Zavarro for her help with the cover typesetting.

INTRODUCTION:
Teenage Nihilist Discovers Alfred Jarry, Runs Amok

When I look back on the suburban angst of my high school years, one surreal scene especially stands out: the vision of myself slumping in the bleachers on the football field during a compulsory pep rally, blissfully perusing *The Selected Works of Alfred Jarry* while all around me countless numbers of my fellow adolescents were engaged in the quaint rite of sacrificing their larynxes to the mindless and bloodthirsty god of "school spirit." Though the ambient noise level was hazardous to hearing, I remained oblivious, remote, contented, an unassailable atoll surrounded by stormy seas but only dimly aware of their furious roar. Let the uncivilized fools revel in their Stone Age amusements; I was content to wander in Jarry's rarified "pataphysical" universe. (Since I wasn't the rah-rah type by any stretch of the imagination, it amuses me no end when I realize that today I am, after a fashion, a Jarry cheerleader. Oh, well—that's pataphysics for you.)

I had stumbled across Jarry's *Selected Works* quite by accident, when I wandered into a local bookstore in the process of cutting class one afternoon. Bored, and probably in some chemically-altered condition or other, I went drifting aimlessly toward the literature section, vaguely hoping to get in a cursory perusal of *Tropic of Cancer* before I was apprehended and evicted by the eternally vigilant management. But I never got to the M's, for, a couple of shelves below, there was *The Selected Works* with its bristling woodcut of Ubu (by no less an artist than Jarry himself). As fate would have it, the first thing to catch my eye when I opened the book was the poem *Tatane*, translated into English as "Nookie." Being fifteen years old, I had a distinctly limited grasp of the vagaries of literature, but I definitely knew what I liked, and poems called "Nookie" were right at the head of that category. However, when I slouched defiantly up to the cash register and attempted to purchase the volume in question, I was informed by the clerk (whose twilight years were undoubtedly being grievously foreshortened by insolent truants like myself) that she couldn't sell it to me. Her logic was internally consistent, if otherwise somewhat open to question: Grove Press published dirty books—they had published *The Selected Works*—ergo, *The Selected Works* must be a dirty book, and of course she had no intention of contributing to the delinquency of a minor, *harrumph*, these kids today, *tsk-tsk*. Pretending to be chagrined, I returned the volume to its rack. But the moment the meddle-some clerk's back was turned, I was out on the street in a flash—furtively hugging the hastily-resnatched tome close to my side, under my sweater. I was a teenage criminal . . .

I don't know what I was expecting when I first began reading Jarry, but it didn't take me very long to become the most enthusiastic (and only) pataphysician on my high school campus. I found something absurdly exhilarating about Jarry's staunch refusal to accept the parameters of "reality," and in his equally stubborn insistence on living in his own personal universe. Born into stultifyingly mundane circumstances, Jarry had succeeded in transforming his existence into a veritable work of ironic art, and had done so with a dashing satirical bravado that had as much courage in it as humor. I was especially struck by the *way* he had refashioned his life, choosing to regard it as a grotesque puppet show with himself in center stage—the most bizarre marionette who ever bewildered a world irrevocably locked into the cut-and-dried and the predictable. Since no one—not even an Alfred Jarry—can flout the immutable laws of society and remain unscathed, there was only one possible punch line to the ridiculous joke of his life, and that was an early and ignominious death. Yet Jarry had remained in character right to the bitter end—marching fiercely off into eternity with an ironic sneer, accompanied by the asthmatic discord of an imaginary calliope and the tinny crash of cheap cymbals.

But I was impressed by more than the surface theatricality of Jarry's brief life. Reading his eloquent, paradoxically subtle and brazen writing, I could sense how desperately he had sought to transcend the bewildering contradictions inherent in human existence. "The soul is a tic," he had groaned as he wrestled with the polarities of vulgarity and purity, scientific reasoning and mystical speculation. Pataphysics, his "science of imaginary solutions," was his attempt to contain all his highly contradictory urges under one enormous, billowing circus tent without attempting to harmonize any of their discord. Realizing this, it was easy to appreciate the all-too-human torment that lay just beneath his brusque, often brutal, exterior.

Finally, when I discovered that Jarry had written the original version of his best-known work, the play *Ubu Roi* (or *Ubu the King*), as a satire on his bourgeois and fatuous high school physics professor, I was hooked. From that point onward, my own high school career became more and more pataphysical and rebellious until I was finally dismissed from my studies, rather curtly and without benefit of diploma, a year early; apparently the administration was more concerned about my noxious influence on other students than it was with its own pedagogic obligations. I didn't mind at all, even if this academic failure ultimately sealed my doom—the only career open to an unlettered idiot savant like myself being the highly erratic one of writing.

Jarry was always perched on the edge of my unconscious when I wrote, a truculent intellectual guru armed with loaded pistols and a fencing foil. He was a dogged taskmaster, too: whenever anything even faintly maudlin or sentimental threatened to creep into my work, he would rattle his imaginary saber warningly and growl in his characteristic monotone, "E-mo-tion-al out-bursts are ex-treme-ly un-pat-a-phys-i-cal." As my (self-appointed) patron saint of Pataphysics, he admonished me always to keep an eye peeled for the exception, never the rule. Under the trenchant tutelage of this nihilistic animus, my output became uniformly singular, if not so uniformly saleable.

Over the years I was always anxious to foist off Jarry's exploits and opinions on friends, neighbors, chance acquaintances on public conveyances—anyone who would stand still long enough to listen. But despite the fact that Jarry had left an indelible imprint on 20th-century literature and art, I rarely encountered anyone else who had even heard of him. In fact, one good friend of mine, Lincoln Haynes, a newspaperman and writer, actually accused me of fabricating Jarry from the pataphysical cloth of my deranged mind. (Haynes only recanted when the Los Angeles *Times* carried a lengthy review of a production of *Ubu Roi*—and only after he had satisfied himself that I hadn't written the review under a pseudonym.) I soon reached the conclusion that Jarry had to be one of the best-kept secrets of 20th-century literature. Even the blurb on the back cover of *The Selected Works* started out with the perhaps rhetorical but ultimately unsettling question, "Who was Alfred Jarry?" If the editors of his selected works didn't know who he was, then who the hell *did* know—besides me, of course?

This book, then, is my attempt to answer that question. Considering the volatile world situation, and Jarry's role as "the first sublime humorist of the Apocalypse," now seems as good a time as any to bring the little shrimp back onstage to gleefully point out a few more of our all-too-human failings. For despite his sideshow trappings and deliberately outrageous behavior, Jarry was actually a profoundly serious writer, concerned with the largest and most timeless issues—the horrors of human greed and rapacity, the multitude of ways in which it is possible to perceive reality, the relationship between mere man and the powers of the universe, the unfathomable mysteries of sex, and the ultimate perfectability of mankind. As a human being and as a writer, Alfred Jarry experienced both darkness and light; his genius lay in his staunch refusal to see the one as separate from the other, and in his burning desire to push past the perceptual obstacles that tie us to the mundanity of the familiar and prevent us from soaring out into infinity. In his life, he almost made it; in his writing, he succeeded beyond a doubt. Lurking somewhere in the personal legend of his life and the literary mythology of his writing was a genuine human being, perhaps small in stature but certainly enormous intellectually. So if you'll please step this way, ladies and gentlemen, I'd like to introduce him to you now—only watch out, he's been known to bite . . .

N.L.
September 8, 1983
(110th anniversary of Alfred Jarry's birth)

Alfred Jarry:
The Man with the Axe

Born Behind the Eight Ball

The circumstances which attended the birth of Alfred Jarry, absurdist author supreme, were so parochial and ridiculous that their product was destined to spend the rest of his short life attempting to obliterate them. Along the way he also managed to trash, torch, and hatchet vast expanses of 19th century morality, almost as an afterthought. Jarry, of course, was hardly the first exceptional mind ever born into a mediocre environment, but his reaction to that environment went beyond mere reflex to extend into the rarified realm of literature. From this end of time, we can only commend him for the thoroughness as well as the originality of his approach.

It has been duly recorded that Alfred-Henri Jarry made his first appearance in this best of all possible worlds at 5:00 A.M. on September 8, 1873—an event which happened to fall on the Feast of the Nativity of the Blessed Virgin. He was born in the village of Laval, Mayenne province, a stone's throw from the boundary of Brittany. Those who attach undue importance to birth order should take note: Alfred was the third and last child of Anselme Jarry and his wife, Caroline, *née* Quernest. The rest of

Madame Jarry's maiden name had been Trernec'h de Coutouly de Dorset, and she was of Breton ancestry, a fact which was to have a marked effect on her son's life and writing.

As for Anselme Jarry, he was later to be dismissed by his only son as "an unimportant bugger." Whether this was deserved or not, Anselme can truthfully be regarded as a French Willy Loman, a well-meaning but ineffectual bourgeois whose life serves as a textbook illustration of the old cliche, "The road to hell is paved with good intentions." He had been born in 1837 into a family who had for untold generations lived stolidly and sluggishly in the villages of Grenoux and Louverné near Laval without any apparent desire to see other parts of the world or even of France. Anselme, however, had raised a few eyebrows in Laval with his sole gesture of independence: when the time came for him to choose a trade, he had abandoned the family occupations of carpentry and masonry to embark upon the exciting life of a traveling textile salesman.

Being thus *forced* to travel, he had crossed over the boundary line of safety and had actually entered Brittany—something, it must be said, that no other member of his family had ever done. Once there, in the town of Hédé, near Rennes, he met Caroline Quernest, five years his junior, who was doomed to become his wife. He realized at once that as marriage material she offered some distinct advantages; her father was a wealthy justice of the peace, a cultured and educated gentleman, and her family could boast, in true Breton fashion, of a long line of noble ancestors. She was a little on the short side, it was true, and there were some serious skeletons in her family closet: both her mother and brother had been confined in asylums for insanity. But Caroline herself had never exhibited any certifiably psychotic tendencies. She had, perhaps unfortunately, received what for that time and place was considered an overly liberal education, and she consequently played the piano and read with a Bovary-like passion which was looked upon with some misgiving by the locals, who believed that a woman's place was in the kitchen or attending Mass. However, Caroline's family's wealth and social position made Anselme Jarry regard these irregularities lightly, and since Caroline's parents were relieved to be able to marry off their eccentric and headstrong daughter, the unlikely pair were joined together in holy matrimony on July 16, 1865, thereafter to make their home in Laval.

It was not destined to be a marriage made in heaven. The Jarrys' first child, a daughter named Caroline-Marie and called Charlotte, was born on February 8, 1868. There was no further issue until 1872, when a son was born who died shortly thereafter. Then, during the birth of Alfred a year later, Mme. Jarry suffered injuries which meant that this would be the last of her children. Anselme, meanwhile, had begun to experience serious business reverses. At first his career had seemed to be in the ascendancy, for he was rapidly promoted from peripatetic salesman to full partner in the Laval textile factory owned by a M. Marie. However, Anselme must have reverted to the phlegmatic behavior of his ancestors under pressure (with detrimental effects on his on-the-job performance), for by the time Alfred was a few months old, Anselme was nearly bankrupt. The family finances forced him to resume his old salesman's job, and the ignominy of the demotion consequently drove him to drink. Thereafter he could often be found in Laval's wretched tavern, drowning his sorrows in alcohol: a sad but noble sight as he struggled with the impossible burden which Fate had so cruelly allotted to him. He was supported in his desperate and bourgeois dipsomania by the equally alcoholic townsmen of Laval, who buttressed his rationales by agreeing that he was, after all, a man impoverished through no fault of his own, and married to a veritable madwoman as well.

There is no denying that Mme. Jarry often exhibited tendencies bordering on the bizarre, or behavior which was at least viewed as such by the good townspeople of Laval. Instead of staying quietly at home and tending to the upbringing of her children, raising them to be pious Catholics and rightfully suspicious of such dangerous influences as literature and music, Caroline Jarry was a maverick. She put a strain on the family budget by insisting on buying a piano; she read books, which in itself was suspicious. Most embarrassingly, she took to the streets in what can charitably be called quaint clothing. (Alfred was later to recall one occasion when she dressed up as a Spanish toreador, complete with short velvet jacket and cap—all the better to perform her usual function of taking the bull by the horns, no doubt.)

But worst of all was the way she berated her poor husband in a strident and tactless manner for his lack of business sense. She insisted on telling him every move to make—often in public. Rather than fight her openly, he merely increased the frequency and amount of his drinking. Sooner or later, whatever veneer of domestic equilibrium that had ever existed in the Jarry domicile was bound to crack, and to the surprise of no one, it eventually did. The ostensible reason was young Alfred's education.

In May 1878, Alfred had started school in Laval. From the very beginning, he showed signs of being a promising and even an exceptional student, much to his mother's delight. (Another thing that gave the Laval villagers plenty to gossip about was the indulgent manner in which Mme. Jarry treated her only son. Her daughter Charlotte occupied a considerably less exalted position in the family, receiving treatment more usually reserved for scullery maids and other emptiers of slop buckets.) But since Laval was such a cultural and intellectual backwater, its educational facilities were hardly fit to prepare Alfred for the brilliant intellectual future his mother envisioned for him. Since she herself had little to look forward to in the town, she was doubly determined that her only son

should not fall into the same trap by becoming a carpenter, mason, or businessman *manqué* in the family tradition. Alfred's only ticket out of oblivion, she realized, was to attend a university, and he wasn't likely to pass a university's competitive entrance examinations if he continued studying in Laval.

Therefore, when Alfred had just turned six, Caroline Jarry collected him and his sister and, leaving her husband behind in Laval, moved to the coastal town of Saint-Brieuc in Brittany, where her father had just retired. No doubt she was glad to remove herself from the stifling strictures of Laval and the depressing spectacle of Anselme day by day approaching ever nearer to a drunkard's grave. As for Anselme's reaction to the departure of his wife and children, it can only be surmised, for he was apparently so taciturn that his opinions on the subject were never even tendered, much less recorded. At any rate, he was to play no further role in the molding of the character of his exceptional young son. As Alfred Jarry described the pitiful old *paterfamilias* a number of years later (by which time his figures of speech had become drolly bombastic and bloated with the "royal 'we' ''): "Our father was an unimportant bugger—what you might call a good old boy (*un bien brave homme*). He certainly created our older sister, an 1830-style girl who liked wearing ribbons in her hair, but he can't have had much to do with the confection of our precious person!"

In Saint-Brieuc, away from the embarrassing spectacle of the "good old boy," Alfred became a veritable whiz kid in his studies. During the school year of 1886, for instance, he took prizes in Latin, English, and French composition; two years later he added further awards to his collection in Greek, German, geography, physical science, mathematics, and drawing. No doubt with the blessings of his mother, he also learned the Breton language, an undertaking which was fraught with peril since the French government—hoping to quell the Breton movement then afoot to secede from France and establish an autonomous republic—had made it illegal for anyone to speak Breton. Jarry admired the Bretons for their independence, and despite this prohibition, he became fluent in the language of his mother's ancestors. The Celtic nuances of that ancient tongue subsequently lent their incantational properties to much of his later writing, especially his poetry, which would have a number of Breton words and allusions to Breton landscapes in it. (Jack Kerouac, also of Breton ancestry, was another modern writer whose writing was influenced by the Breton language in one way or another.)

There was something surreal about the Breton countryside that both fascinated and depressed young Jarry; he despised it for its murky, eerie bleakness but found himself drawn to it just the same. Rugged, isolated, and marshy, it was at once mysterious and sullen, a bizarre commingling of paleolithic ruins, Gothic architecture, and maritime geography, all blanketed in perpetual mist. In an early poem, "St.-Brieuc the Cabbage Patch," written in May 1886, Jarry described the village as being "two leagues from the sea, two steps from manure piles . . . Ah, what a miserable place." Always a loner, Alfred was given to taking long walks across the countryside, jotting down fragments of poems and stories while he walked. Not only did he have a definite bent for writing, but he kept at it with a doggedness that bordered on ferocity: after producing his first piece of youthful scribbling in 1885, during the next four years he went on to produce nine plays and thirty-three poems.

His personality was already beginning to solidify at the age of twelve. The French, as they often seem to do, have a word which describes the young Jarry perfectly—*farouche*, which indicates a combination of wildness, fierceness, sullenness, and shyness. His ferocity came, no doubt, from attempting to compensate for the fact that his parents were separated (a serious social stigma in rural France) and also for his own unprepossessing appearance. The unfortunate lad had inherited his mother's short stature as well as her keen intellect, and his attitude of seeming unconcern and disaffection masked the underlying uncertainty and embarrassment he must have felt by appearing a physical and intellectual freak to his schoolmates. He had learned early in life that the best protection against ridicule was a sharply cutting remark, shot forth before his opponent had a chance to attack him, and he never failed to employ this tactic. As a result, his fellow students soon learned to leave him alone. Luckily, he was also capable of making friends, and he showed a touching loyalty towards the few boys he considered his intimates. This was a trait he would possess throughout his life; his closest friends would always be those who were wise enough to look beneath his seemingly unbroachable exterior and see the suffering midget beneath the enormous hide of arrogance that sheltered him. For his part, despite a fundamental eccentricity that grew by leaps and bounds over the years until it eventually swallowed him whole, Jarry always stood staunchly by his friends, perhaps appreciating their ability to accept him as he was. It was a touching quality, shining through his later behavioral excesses and providing a glimpse into his basic nature.

In the autumn of 1888, Caroline Jarry packed up her brood and the Jarry *ménage* moved its base of operations to the nearby town of Rennes so that Alfred could begin cramming for the university at the Rennes *lycée*, or prep school. Nobody would have suspected it at the time, but Jarry's experiences in Rennes were destined to both enlarge and transcend his

boyish misanthropy until, in its adult form, it would eventually topple the smug world of 19th-century literature from its throne and send it sprawling on its fat posterior.

Pataphysics 101

No doubt the young Jarry's first view of the Rennes *lycée* was more than a little disconcerting. Classes were held in the dank and dismal ruins of a 17th-century convent; the atmosphere of decay was all-pervasive. Henri Hertz, a classmate of Jarry's at the time, recalled part of the dubious environment thusly: "The physics classes were taught in the old buildings. The plaster was falling off the walls and ceilings, the tables for the experiments were warped, and the corners were dirty."

Jarry lost no time in acclimatizing himself to his new surroundings, however. In short order, he had studiously acquired an iconoclastic and flamboyant reputation in order to deflect attention from his ignominious social position and peculiar appearance. For, to put it bluntly, he was hardly the heroic type. Hertz no doubt stated the case accurately when he recalled that, "We called him 'Quasimodo.'" The unfortunate lad remained extremely short in stature, barely five feet tall (a height he would never exceed), with "a forehead like a rock," a voice which "'cut' in all senses of the word," and a peculiar gait which, with his bowlegs, said Hertz, made Jarry look like "a fat bird walking." "In the *lycée* and in the town he had a reputation which, in family circles and among professors, provoked sudden silence and obvious embarrassment," Hertz observed. "At any mention of his irregularities, his escapades, and to tell the whole truth his vices, parents lowered their voices and children their eyes."

Despite his penchant for reputedly unsavory activities and behavioral anarchy, Jarry continued to be an exemplary student and thus he was rarely, if ever, reprimanded for his disruptive shenanigans. Nearly everyone at the *lycée*, both students and professors, was basically intimidated by his sharp intellect and trenchant wit. It was a perilous undertaking to attempt to challenge Jarry; his keen mind and cutting responses under such circumstances soon became legendary. Hertz summed up the situation succinctly: "He was a brilliant student with all the marks of the worst kind of troublemaker. He excelled in his studies but without trying." During the school year of 1889, for instance, he won awards in chemistry, French composition, German, Latin, and Greek.

Unlike his fellow sweathogs at Rennes, he treated study as if it were a hobby. He had many interests in the sciences—he devoured the latest research papers by noted scientific minds the way his schoolmates dug into serialized adventure novels—and he also continued his own forays into the world of literature. His literary interests were wide-ranging and included Rabelais, Goethe (especially *Faust*), Coleridge, Shakespeare, and classic Latin and Greek texts. (But he was disgusted by the universality of Voltaire, whose books he often satirized). His particular favorite was Isidore Ducasse, the "Comte de Lautrèamont," whose *Chants de Maldoror*, with its savage misanthropy and violent imagery, was to have a profound and lasting influence on his own work.

As for his own writing, he continued to produce a great deal of it, from mock-heroic dramas to scatological satires on his teachers and fellow students. Teenage parody is a time-honored student temptation, of course, but true to form, Jarry took this juvenile tomfoolery one step beyond and attempted to satirize his professors in a far more ambitious fashion than was generally the case. It was plain that his was an astoundingly original sort of intellect, even though it was also apparent that at least part of this originality stemmed from Jarry's alarmingly misanthropic tendencies, which were already fully developed despite his youth.

It has been noted, however, that Jarry also possessed an outgoing and loyal side to his personality. Although he had little interest in becoming a student leader or in otherwise supporting what he viewed as bourgeois educational ideals (the modern idea of "school spirit" would no doubt have nauseated him), he thoroughly enjoyed the companionship of a number of his contemporaries at the *lycée*. In addition to Henri Hertz, he also struck up a friendship with Henri Morin, a boy his own age. Theirs was a partnership which was to have a profound effect on the future of modern literature.

About halfway through Jarry's sojourn in the Rennes *lycée*, he and Henri Morin began collaborating on a play, the chief character of which was a caricature of professor Félix Hébert. Hébert had the misfortune to teach physics at the *lycée* in the decrepit "classroom" described by Hertz. A corpulent, fundamentally incompetent academic baboon with a pale, porcine face, small eyes, and a blonde moustache, Hebert had inspired an almost mythical disgust in his students; he was the professor all the boys loved to hate. They brought him thoughtful little presents of grasshoppers, frogs, and other savory livestock; they blatantly neglected their studies during class in order to draw charming "portraits" of Hébert's grotesque form (Jarry himself made a number of such drawings); and they took great pleasure in composing extravagant satires on his ponderous and pretentious academese (he was given to describing his subject as "my science of physics"). In short, they made Hebert's life perennially distracting, if not particularly pleasant.

For Alfred Jarry, this was a tailor-made situation. His brilliant and dwarfish misanthropy rose spectacularly to the delightful occupation of tormenting Professor Hébert—"Père Heb" or "Père Hébe" as the boys sneeringly called him to his face. When the hapless Heb was foolish enough to call upon Alfred in the classroom, "Quasimodo" responded with a long, rambling monologue which incorporated Attic Greek apostrophes and Rabelaisian smut, among other things. In the face of such an convoluted and intellectually dazzling assault, the other students were convulsed and the faint-hearted Heb reduced almost to tears. After a few such encounters with the midget *enfant terrible*, Heb rapidly learned the wisdom of leaving Jarry alone.

Henri Morin was in Jarry's physics class during this period, and the two boys soon became good friends. Not too long after this, Morin showed Jarry the play, *The Poles* (*Les Polonais*), which Morin and his brother Charles had written to satirize the luckless and graceless Hébert about a year before Jarry had come to Rennes. Before Jarry got his hands on it, *The Poles* was your basic schoolboy satire—hardly an original piece of writing. Its plot was lifted in haste from Shakespeare's *Macbeth*. It portrayed Hébert (called Père Heb in the play) as a rapacious fool out to take over a world of which he understood less than nothing, a one-dimensional figure in front of a cardboard backdrop.

Once Jarry became interested in the project, however, the play became decidedly more bizarre. In accord with Jarry's eclectic intellectual interests, Heb became a truly monstrous character, half buffoon and half archetype. He was described, for instance, as having an enormous and all-encompassing belly (*gidouille*, from the word *ouiller*, meaning to refill an empty barrel) with concentric circles ringing his umbilical section and representing simultaneous states of emptiness and greed. (Hébert, the empty-headed bourgeois, was forever stuffing himself with sweets.) Heb was also said to have three teeth (one of stone, one of iron, one of wood) and a single ear, which was retractable.

After Jarry and Henri Morin had made all these changes in *The Poles*, they decided to stage the play using some marionettes Jarry had received as a Christmas present. Jarry's sister Charlotte built the papier-mache puppet of Père Heb, basing her design on the absurd physique of Hébert himself, whom she had seen passing by the Jarry home. Jarry constructed and painted the sets (along with his other talents, he showed some promise as an artist) and spoke the lines of the play's protagonist during the actual performance. The world premiere of *The Poles* took place in December 1888, in the Morins' attic. Jarry referred to this homespun venue as the "Théâtre des Phynances," no doubt making an ironic comment on the lack thereof; subsequent performances of *The Poles* were held under his own roof.

There was not a large audience at the first performance of the play; Mme. Jarry supplied the little troupe with piano accompaniment for their talent show, and the whole thing would probably have passed into adolescent obscurity if Père Heb hadn't been destined to play a much larger

role in Jarry's life and thinking. In his bloated mindlessness, Heb typified everything Jarry was rapidly growing to hate—smug, self-satisfied bourgeois mediocrity; intellectual sluggishness; and hypocrisy. Eventually, Jarry would become virtually obsessed with the Heb archetype, writing more and more about him until the bombastic figure of this miserable clown finally took on the proportions of an anti-heroic legend. But all this was still a few years away; meanwhile, Heb simmered on the back burner of Jarry's consciousness, a noxious soufflé that was growing fatter and more gross by the hour.

Jarry's student life was not all intellectual. He enjoyed lighter amusements as well—fencing, hiking, and bicycling being among his favorite pastimes. Always flamboyant, perhaps because it diverted attention away from his basically introverted nature, Jarry was often the ringleader of expeditions where he and his friends would don outlandish garb and terrorize the citizenry in beautiful downtown Rennes. Sometimes Jarry and his cohorts would dress up as swordsmen and stage fierce mock assaults on the vendors in the marketplace. At other times Jarry and Henri Morin would put on monks' habits and stroll through the town looking properly contemplative, but occasionally letting some extremely unmonklike language pass their lips. Then there were bicycle excursions to Mont.-St.-Michel, or daylong tramps across the countryside to view some ancient ruins or a bit of medieval architecture.

Jarry was always extremely active, burning the candle at both ends with his studies and amusements. Sometimes he would arrive late for his first class of the day, looking drawn and disheveled, with dark circles under his eyes which pointed incontrovertibly to a sleepless night. When asked where he had been, he would state flatly in his characteristically cutting and metallic voice: ''In the brothels.'' No one doubted him.

From Nowhere to Paris by Bicycle

Although Jarry's academic record at the Rennes *lycée* had been outstanding, he was soon to discover that it was one thing to be a whiz kid in a one-horse town like Rennes, and quite another to make his mark in the world of serious academia. In the fall of 1890, again complying with his mother's wishes, he stopped studying at the Rennes *lycée* in order to cram for the entrance exam into the Ecole Normale Supérieure in Paris. This university, highly regarded throughout France, had room for only twenty-five new applicants from all of France each year, and the rigors of its entrance examinations were legendary. Precisely how rigorous they were became apparent when Jarry, after taking the exams, received his test scores that July: in all his subjects he had failed to even remotely approach the university's requirements for admittance!

It was obvious that he was never going to accumulate sufficient knowledge in Rennes to enable him to compete with France's most brilliant students for those twenty-five annual vacancies at the Ecole Normale Supérieure; thus, in the fall of 1891, he was bid a tearful farewell by Mme. Jarry and packed off to the *Lycée* Henri IV in Paris, there to beef up his academic requirements. He was seventeen years old.

At this point, in keeping with the growingly cartoonish tendencies of Jarry's life, the details take on an exaggerated, larger-than-life quality. We see our seventeen-year-old hero pumping resolutely into Paris on his bicycle, a fierce, shy, and witty midget with the salt air of the marshy Breton outback still clinging to his ragged cyclist's clothes. We see him, characteristically unimpressed with life in the big city, striding purposefully through the halls of the *Lycée* Henri IV, an eccentric but ironically witty and literate young savage wearing a swirling, floor-length black cape and a tall black stovepipe hat—"a veritable observatory dome," according to one of his fellow students—which nearly exceeds Jarry's own altitude. We catch a glimpse of him when, during lunch hour, he is challenged by a group of fellow students to improvise a speech on the most arbitrary subject they can dream up—Turkistan! Jarry obliges by launching into a long and brilliant monologue which touches on a universe of tangents, from Aziade to Pierre Loti, thoroughly mystifying his listeners. When pressed to stick to the subject, he indignantly cites Cicero as having set a precedent in digressing during the course of a public speech, and then resumes his harangue, having effectively silenced his critics. He grinds to a halt only when the bell rings, signaling the end of the lunch period.

It was behavior of this type that led Jarry's contemporaries to extravagant appraisals of his actions—appraisals which not only added to the rapidly growing Jarry mythos, but which no doubt encouraged Jarry to become even more *outré* and bizarre. As long as no one saw beneath the caricature of his eccentric persona, he was safe from judgement. If his behavior made people think he

was an unsavory character, so much the better; at least no one was likely to mistake him for a recent arrival from the staid world of the bourgeoisie!

A characteristic reaction to Jarry's eccentricities was presented by one of the students who was present during Jarry's verbal tour of Turkistan, and who was both impressed and disturbed by something maniacal in Jarry: "When he opened the valve of his wit, he seemed to follow after the stream of his words without any control over them. It was no longer a person speaking but a machine driven by some demon. His jerky voice, metallic and nasal, his abrupt puppet-like gestures, his fixed expression, his torrential and incoherent flow of language, his grotesque or brilliant images, this synchronism which today we should compare to the movies or the phonograph—all this astonished me, amused me, irritated me, and ended by upsetting me. [Jarry] was informed, intelligent, and discriminating; he was good, even sweet-tempered, and perhaps timid beneath it all. But he lacked that something which prevents people from putting the cart always before the horse and from ruining their lives. His originality was too much like some mental anomaly." Jarry undoubtedly gloried in such responses to his personal theatrics and was inspired to outdo himself the next time he had an audience—any audience. As a result, the cartoon of his life became more absurd and unreal as time went on, until there would come a nightmarish period when Jarry himself would lose track of just where the convoluted plot of his life—real or imagined—was going. This absurdist *Walpurgisnacht* was still a number of years away, however. Meanwhile, Jarry immersed himself in his studies and in the teeming intellectual life of the capital. It is possible, in fact, that he spent too much time carousing rather than studying, for his second group of scores for the Ecole Normale entry examination, while better than the first, were still inadequate. Some of the blame can be put on the fact that during most of his first year at the Henri IV, Jarry had been living in a dank and drafty attic room in a building near the Boulevard de Port-Royal, located at the foot of a dismal alley too narrow for two people to walk abreast. He humorously called this neo-Gothic apartment the "Dead Man's Calvary." It was decorated with his own woodcuts and with cabalistic drawings; censers hung from the low ceiling, and there were handprints in blood on the outside stairwell. Jarry shared the premises with a couple of pet owls, animals which he admired because of their nocturnal lifestyle and rapacious intelligence—traits which mirrored his own. (At some point after the birds died, he had them stuffed.)

But what was really keeping Jarry from his formal studies was the bubbling intellectual ferment of Paris at the height of *la belle epoque*. His striking intelligence soon gained him entrance into Parisian literary circles, and he began to be a familiar sight at the poet Mallarmé's "at homes" on Thursday afternoons as well as at the Tuesday afternoon receptions held at the offices of the *Mercure de France*, one of the most important literary publications of the period. Distasteful memories of life in the boondocks were quickly left behind as Jarry plunged into the chaotic and exhilarating world of the capital. On all sides, the old order—political, social, and artistic—of the 19th century was visibly and audibly disintegrating; change was in the wind. This tempestuous intellectual climate was perfect for Jarry, to whom idealism had always been a ridiculously bourgeois concept and whose far-reaching intellectual idiosavancy caused him to be highly suspicious of formalized ideologies.

Jarry began causing a stir among the literati with his highly eccentric behavior from the moment he first appeared. It wasn't long before he went from being a rumor in his spare time to becoming a twenty-four-hour literary phenomenon. In the *Mercure de France* salon, hosted at the magazine's offices in the Rue de l'Echaudé by its editor Alfred Vallette and his wife Marguerite Eymery Vallette (who wrote under the pseudonym "Rachilde"), Jarry met many of the greatest writers, artists, and composers of the time. Among them were Catulle Mendès, Félix Fénéon,

Henri de Régnier, Pierre Louÿs, Gustave Kahn, Franc-Nohain, Remy de Gourmont, André Gide, Toulouse-Lautrec, Gauguin, Paul Sèrusier, Henri Rousseau, and Maurice Ravel. The artistic and political ferment of the times was represented by proponents of every conceivable theory and artistic movement: there were Symbolists, Fauvists, decadents, mystics, anarchists, and endless combinations thereof.

Jarry amazed these august personages with his ongoing act; none of them had ever seen anything remotely like it. André Gide described him as "having a plaster-colored complexion, outfitted like a circus clown, playing the role of a fantastically constructed character, resolutely artificial . . . [His manner of speaking was] strange, implacable, without inflection, without nuance, with a style of equally accenting each syllable, including the mute ones. A nutcracker would speak thusly." Soon the frequenters of Parisian literary salons were all attempting to outdo one another with their imitations of Jarry's dress, speech, and mannerisms. But that was impossible—Jarry was easily the most bizarre personage in a universe of bizarre personages.

Rachilde, the novelist wife of the *Mercure*'s editor, Vallette—and the subsequent author of a Jarry biography, *Le surmâle des lettres*, or *The Supermale of Letters*, which is by virtue of its direct and personal approach one of the most valuable documents about Jarry's life, although it has never been translated into English—was immediately struck by Jarry's brusque, idiosyncratic style. She took due note of his "dirty, shabby" dress (on his first visit to the *Mercure* salon, he wore a pair of grubby cyclist's trousers and beat-up canvas shoes from which protuded his very visible toes); his strange manner of speaking (which she described as sounding like "rusted gears meshing"); and his savage, solipsistic way of imposing himself on the situation come hell or high water. (His first charming comment on this particular occasion was, "Idiot! Why aren't you working a spinning-wheel?") As we shall see, he had scant use for women, especially women of letters, although he soon grew very fond of Rachilde nonetheless.

Rachilde soon became equally fascinated with Jarry's razor-sharp intellect, as did her husband. The Vallettes, especially Rachilde, were to be Jarry's staunchest supporters in his times of need—publishers, friends, and on numerous occasions even roommates. A handsome and spirited woman who was proud of the fact that her androgynous pseudonym often made readers of her novels think she was a man, Rachilde found Jarry's seeming sexual inaccessibility a tantalizing mystery. Although he affected a profound dislike of women (and in fact said so in no uncertain terms, announcing to her quite imperiously, "We do not like women at all"), she found something mysteriously attractive in his pale face, bright red lips, long, straight black hair, and "dark, phosphorescent eyes like those of a night bird"—eyes which often, Rachilde observed, flashed like lightning. Jarry had an aura of danger about him which made her think of him as "a man of the woods," a feral creature who broke into the literary world "like a wild animal entering the ring," but who underneath it all was paradoxically reticent to the point of being retiring. There is a possibility that Rachilde and Jarry had an affair; over the years the Vallettes and Jarry shared a number of residences, and it was certainly possible and even routine in those freewheeling times for two literary types

to engage in extracurricular collaborations. Whatever their relationship was based on, however, Jarry remained very close to Rachilde for the duration of his short life, and he even paid her a compliment which he would never have bestowed on any other woman: "Mada-me, your character is nothing to shout about, and like all of us you are a negligible assemblage of atoms. But we will grant you one quality: you don't cling.'' Perhaps the fact that Rachilde was capable of appreciating this left-handed appraisal explains why Jarry was so fond of her; it took an exceptional ability to see beneath the surface of things to understand that sort of badinage.

Another early champion of Jarry's in Paris was Marcel Schwob, editor of the literary supplement to the monthly magazine *L'Echo de Paris*. Schwob was the first editor in Paris to publish Jarry's writing. On April 23, 1893, the *Echo de Paris* featured "Guignol," a short work of prose by Jarry, which had been awarded first prize in the *Echo*'s prose competition. "Guignol" is of interest for a number of reasons, not the least of which is the fact that it introduced a character named Père Ubu (formerly our old friend from the Rennes *lycée*, Père Heb) and a quasi-science called "'Pataphysics.''

A month after the appearance of "Guignol," Jarry also won the *Echo*'s poetry prize for three "prose poems." Not long afterward, he and a friend, writer Léon-Paul Fargue (with whom he shared a room off and on in a squalid hotel, complete with puddles of urine on the pavement out front and a large menagerie of assorted animals in the room itself), soon began contributing to Louis Lormel's *L'Art Litteraire*; other contributors to this journal included Mallarmé, Gide, and Remy de Gourmont.

Jarry and Fargue were the closest of friends; some have even ventured the opinion that they may have been lovers, although in all fairness our boy Alfred seemed as ultimately dubious about homosexual love as he was about the heterosexual variety. As he had done in Rennes with friends like Henri Morin, Jarry continued to enjoy exhibiting flamboyant, *outré* behavior in public. One afternoon Fargue and Jarry sat down in a cafe, and Jarry began lecturing the patrons on the subject of masturbation "from personal recollections.'' Fargue, who, one suspects, was used to serving as Jarry's straight man, then raised the profound question, "What is Art but intellectual masturbation?'' It was a point worth pondering, but history does not record whether or not the cafe's patrons lingered to discuss it any further.

Jarry's sense of exhilaration at becoming part of the Parisian literary world was dampened considerably by a severe bout with influenza which he suffered at the beginning of 1893. His mother and sister immediately came to Paris from Brittany to look after him, and under their care he gradually began to recover, but then Mme. Jarry also became ill with the same ailment. She died on May 10. It was a terrible blow for Jarry, who had loved and respected his mother for her independence and her rebellion against his father, but her death did not prevent him from resolutely taking the Ecole Normale examinations for the second time in July. Once again, he failed to win admission, although his scores were much higher than before. He put his name down to repeat the examinations the following July, but for a number of reasons his days of formal schooling were about to come to a close. The death of Caroline Jarry marked the end of an era in her son's life; it made him realize his own mortality, for one thing, and that in turn increased his already strongly absurdist view of the world. (His most moving novel, *L'Amour Absolu* [*Absolute Love*], would be about the subject of maternal love.) Largely in response to his mother's death, Jarry's behavior continued to grow even more bizarre, and although he had always been prone to drink, he now began to drink more heavily, a trait which was noted with concern by his friends, especially Rachilde. However, this emotional turmoil was also to manifest itself in the form of an outpouring of writing. Despite the adversities in his personal life, Jarry's literary star was on the ascendancy, and it wouldn't be very long before most of Paris would be fully aware of this young savage from Brittany.

Rebellion in the Ranks, or Sgt. Bilko, Where Were You When We Needed You?

Jarry's first full-length book, *The Records of the Black Crest* (*Les minutes de sable memorial*), was published in September, 1894 by the *Mercure de France*. Illustrated with Jarry's own neo-heraldic woodcuts, the book presented a collection of poems and prose, including the prize-winning selections previously published in the *Echo de Paris*.

The Records of the Black Crest showed off Jarry's eclectic tendencies to perfection. Nearly every aspect of his rapidly developing talent was represented, from speculations that mingled science, logic, symbolism, and absurdity ("The Report Explaining the Terrible Accident of February 30, 1891") to feverish chronicles of opium dreams ("Opium") to an attempt to create a recurrent literary reality like that of a phonograph record, complete with a "scratch" that caused part of a paragraph to repeat itself ("Phonograph"). From this earliest published work of Jarry's, many of his later tendencies can be ascertained in embryonic form—neo- and pseudo-scientific speculation, finely-drawn description, and numerous levels of "reality" existing simultaneously, causing the reader to wonder which is the most "real." Misanthropy and the theme of a malevolent God also play important roles in *The Records of the Black Crest*, especially in the play *Haldernablou*, which describes an allegorical homosexual affair between a man and his servant, played out against the backdrop of a cosmos gone berserk. This play, with its shifting constructs of consciousness and its numerous levels of meaning, was indicative of Jarry's ongoing interest in changing the basic concepts of theater, making it less direct and linear, and achieving a final result which resembled the dream state. At the time, theater was still bound to the Aristotelian ideal, with clearly delineated development encompassing a distinct beginning, middle, and end. *Haldernablou* violated these time-honored tenets, with the result that it soon became a very controversial subject in literary circles.

Not all of the *Haldernablou* controversy was literary, however; the greatest part of it turned out to be sexual. Shortly after the appearance of *The Records of the Black Crest*, Louis Lormel, whose personal relations with Jarry had deteriorated into literary name-calling, insinuated that the two male lovers in *Haldernablou*, Haldern and Ablou, were actually Jarry and his good friend Léon-Paul Fargue, and that the play was a reflection of their actual relationship. While it was true that "Haldern" was the Breton form of "Alfred," and that "Ablou" had originally been called "Cameleo," which was Fargue's nickname, it has also been noted that Lormel was the only one of Jarry's contemporaries to accuse him of being a homosexual. However, the controversy served to focus an intense interest on *The Records of the Black Crest*, and Jarry undoubtedly benefited materially from the notoriety.

Jarry continued to amaze the Parisian literary world in other ways as well. A month after the publication of *The Records of the Black Crest*, he and Remy de Gourmont brought out the first edition of *L'Ymagier*, "A Magazine of Engravings." Although his reputation as a writer was burgeoning, Jarry had never lost his interest in the visual arts, as evidenced by his woodcuts in *The Records of the Black Crest*. The focus of *L'Ymagier* was primarily on religious and grotesque art, with Jarry contributing a goodly number of woodcuts under the name "Alain Jans" as well as writing the commentary on the various engravings. *L'Ymagier* continued to appear monthly until October 1895 at which time Jarry and Gourmont severed their personal and business relationship as a result of a peculiar

event—Jarry seduced, or was seduced by, Gourmont's mistress, who was old enough to be Jarry's mother. However, during the year it had been in existence, *L'Ymagier* had made an important statement about the artistic value of engravings, and as a result of Jarry's missionary work in that line, the art form experienced something of a rebirth.

Although his relationships with Lormel and Gourmont were stormy, Jarry also had a number of friends and protégés whom he went out of his way to help in their careers. One of these was the painter Henri Rousseau—"the Douanier ("Customs Agent") Rousseau"—whose only known lithograph, *La guerre*, was published by Jarry in the second issue of *L'Ymagier*. Jarry had met Rousseau at the *Mercure* salon and had taken a liking to him, perhaps because they both came from Laval. At a time

when Rousseau was being sneered at by the public and derided by his fellow artists as a crude and naive artistic fraud, Jarry stood staunchly behind him, championing his work and attempting to get his paintings into shows in Paris. In return, Rousseau painted Jarry's portrait and gave him refuge in his flat at a time when the impecunious author happened to be out of funds. Jarry's support of the Douanier was not without influence on the opinions of the artists and writers of Paris, and although the genius of Rousseau's work didn't become apparent until after his death, Alfred Jarry deserves a great deal of credit for ensuring that the Douanier didn't pass into total obscurity before he could gain recognition. Ironically, Jarry himself was never much of an admirer of Rousseau's style; he supported the Douanier from an objective viewpoint, realizing that in his painting Rousseau was presenting an entirely new perspective, one which deserved to be preserved for posterity.

Jarry's life took a distinctly unfavorable turn when, in November 1894, he was drafted into the French army—much to his boredom and disgust. He had been successful on two or three prior occasions at slipping out of the suffocating grip of the military, but on November 13, he received an ominous summons from which there was no appeal—he was to report to Laval for immediate induction. Reluctantly, he left Paris and his multifarious intellectual pursuits, and proceeded to Laval.

It should be pointed out that although Jarry's intellect was incredibly far-reaching, he was never very well-informed when it came to politics and history. The Franco-Prussian War of 1870 had failed to make any significant impact either on Jarry or on his thinking. As he observed in 1897 in an essay: "Since I was born in 1873, the war of 1870 is in my mind three years beyond the completely forgotten. It really seemed to me that this event had never occurred, and was simply a pedagogic invention feeding scholarly battalions." Thus, his objection to military life had more to do with its relentless annihilation of individuality than with any political views he might have held. Still, in an era when no one had ever heard of a conscientious objector, he managed to make quite a nuisance of himself.

One wonders just what Jarry's commanding officer thought the first time the stunted, grotesque figure appeared, wearing a new uniform that billowed off his pint-sized frame like a canvas over a tent pole. With his shoulder-length black hair and pale, chalky complexion, Jarry certainly did not appear to be acceptable material for the rigors of army life. The captain, whose name was Bouilly, had specialized in breaking seeming incorrigibles like Jarry for many years, and he must have smiled sadistically to himself as he thought of whipping this imbecile into shape.

"Name, soldier?" he snapped.

It is safe to assume that Bouilly had never experienced anything in his years of basic training to prepare him for Jarry's response. With an outward show of extreme respect—almost servility—Jarry replied in a mechanical voice, speaking in a singsong manner with one syllable high-pitched, the next low-pitched, and the overall result resembling a primitive chant: ''Yes Mon-sieur my nam-eh is Al-fred Jar-ry I am-meh or-ig-in-al-ly a na-tive of La-val and man-neh of let-ters from-meh Par-is.''

Trying not to show that he was thunderstruck, the captain ordered Jarry never to call a superior officer ''Monsieur''—to which the diabolical ''grunt'' answered, ''Ver-ry well Mon-sieur. Here-af-ter I shall call you my cap-tain.'' That was, as might be imagined, only the beginning. In an intelligent and totally anarchistic manner, Jarry declared war on the army, and after a few weeks it appeared as though the army was definitely losing the battle and maybe even the war. Rather than being obviously uncooperative and obnoxious, Jarry continually appeared respectful to the point of obsequiousness, but everywhere he went he nonetheless created havoc and anarchy. During target practice, he utilized his skill with a rifle, along with his sublime sense of the absurd, and managed to reduce the ranks to helpless laughter, often ending the session prematurely with his inappropriate potshots. At drills he was invariably the center of attention, with his robotlike and equally inappropriate motions making him seem like a parody of the perfect soldier. It was little wonder that his superiors soon excused him from drills and parades; they couldn't figure out whether he was mentally deranged or merely a total imbecile—nor could they decide just what to do with him. He ended up swabbing out

latrines, peeling potatoes, and sweeping the parade grounds—all of which menial duties kept him out of sight of the other soldiers and less prone to making deadly attacks on company morale. Even so, Jarry was not daunted; from his vantage point behind his broom, he made sweeping observations: "It is no mere bow to rhetoric to designate with the word 'brush' these objects generally known in the civilian world as brooms. They are, in reality, exceptionally suited for sketching decorative designs on the ground and for roughing out the possible boundaries of a future sweeping project—one which remains highly improbable."

After a few months of this sort of life, Jarry became badly depressed and, longing to be out in the world again, injected himself with picric acid, which turned his skin an intriguing yellow color and baffled the military medics. He was placed in sick bay for a couple of weeks and finally given an honorable discharge, ostensibly for "chronic lithiasis" (gallstones), but in actuality, at least according to Jarry, for "precocious imbecility." He returned immediately to Paris, although the discharge was not declared official until December 14, 1895.

Exactly what effect Jarry had on the French army can only be imagined; but the effect the army had on him was made very clear in his novel, *Days and Nights: A Novel of a Deserter*, which was published in 1897. The book is one of Jarry's most haunting works, since it deals directly and personally with his disdain toward the suffocating military environment and with his constant desire to expand his level of consciousness above that of the mundane. The novel's chief character is Sengle (the name originating from the same Latin root as the word "singular"), a new

recruit who is so brutalized by the mindlessness and violence around him that he is driven to seek release from reality by escaping into a dream world.

There is little question that Jarry's experiences in the army greatly intensified his absurdist and misanthropic tendencies. Again and again in *Days and Nights*, Jarry reveals his disgust with the stupidity of the military. Channeled into the play *Ubu Roi*, that disgust was to create an explosion from which drama and literature would never fully recover. Pa Ubu, adjusting his Polish army uniform, was waiting in the wings for the cue to make his grand entrance.

Ubu Roi, Low Budget Revolutionary

When Jarry arrived in Paris in 1891, he had with him the manuscript of the play *The Poles*, which he had written with Henri and Charles Morin in Rennes. As previously mentioned, *The Poles* was a nasty little schoolboy farce lampooning M. Hébert, the sluggish, ineffectual, bourgeois physics teacher at the Rennes *lycée*. The flimsy plot of this piece of juvenile parody depended very heavily on the cannibalization of *Macbeth*, and on Emanuel Chabrier's comic opera *Le roi malgré lui* ("The King in Spite of Himself"), and no one would have ever suspected that *The Poles* had any future as a serious theater work designed to be presented before a paying audience of adults—and intellectual adults at that.

However, Alfred Jarry never did anything the way he was supposed to, and his career as a playwright was to prove no exception. The figure of "Père Heb," gross caricature of M. Hébert and handy catch-all for all the horrific mediocrities of bourgeois life, had been looming in the back of Jarry's subconscious ever since his time in Rennes. Gradually, as Jarry began to expand his circle of interests and intellectual passions, Père Heb had come to represent, and in fact to sum up, everything Jarry hated about the class into which he had been born: greed (embodied by Heb's enormous belly, which he was forever stuffing with sweets), mediocrity (typified by his ineffectuality), and mindless tyranny over those below him. During his studies at the Lycée Henri IV, Jarry managed to find time to rework *The Poles*, refining its schoolboyish elements and making it more universal. In the course of these revisions, Père Heb acquired a new name—Père Ubu.

The origin of the name Ubu remains murky; it has been suggested that Jarry, with his fluency in Latin, took it from the Latin word *ybex*, meaning vulture. Another theory claims that Jarry was inspired to name his evil character after the ominous call of the predatory owls who shared his dismal quarters with him. Still others insist that the name "Ubu" was a logical development—from Eb to Ebé to Hébé to Heb to Ubu. Everything in Jarry's life is open to speculation, but whatever dark swamp of depravity ultimately spawned the odious name of Ubu matters but little. The atavistic evil of that name merely exists, resonating deep within our primitive selves like the blood-curdling music of a maniac's laughter.

The name and the character are one; it seems likely that they created one another.

Ubu had made his first appearance in print in "Guignol" in 1893, infesting the premises of a scholarly gentleman named Achras and wreaking havoc on Achras' settled life. (Trivia fans take note: Achras, which means "pear tree" in Greek, was the not-so-fond nickname the Rennes troublemakers bestowed on another of their unfortunate teachers, a M. Pèrier.) The following year, in 1894, Ubu reappeared with far more definition in Jarry's play *Caesar Antichrist*, a complex drama which further delineated Jarry's elaborate cosmology of hopelessly foolish mankind and bestial, irrational God. The "Terrestrial" act of *Caesar Antichrist*, devoted to the escapades of Ubu, is essentially a heavily rewritten version of *The Poles*, hung on a demonic and cabalistic framework which lifts it out of the category of schoolboy farce and into the realm of the visionary.

Now began a chain of events which would end with Ubu stomping across the face of of the 19th century in his hobnailed boots. In the spring

of 1896, Jarry's friend Paul Fort prevailed upon him to complete a full-length version of Ubu's exploits, which was published in the review *Le Livre d'Art* under the title *Ubu Roi*. It appeared in book form the following June, with the ironic subtitle "Drama in five acts restored in its entirety as performed at the Théâtre des Phynances in 1885." It wasn't too long after this that Jarry, as an author with a growing reputation among the literary and dramatic cognoscenti of Paris, struck up an acquaintance with Lugné-Poe, director of the Théâtre de l'Oeuvre. Jarry had been following the progress of this drama group with great interest ever since its inception; it was considered to be the most avant-garde company in Paris, with one foot in the Symbolist camp and the other in the anarchistic. One thing led to another, and that summer Lugné-Poe asked Jarry to become his man-of-odd-jobs while he went on vacation.

Jarry proved very conscientious in discharging his various duties, which included forwarding manuscripts to his employer and doing general office work as well as painting scenery (along with artists such as Toulouse-Lautrec and Edward Munch), playing bit parts when necessary, and (most importantly) helping Lugné-Poe schedule the repertory for the upcoming season. Almost immediately, he began attempting to sell Lugné-Poe on the idea of producing *Ubu Roi*. One letter which he wrote to his boss, outlining the virtues of staging *Ubu*, has come to rest in the vault of posterity. In it, Jarry mentions a number of times how cheap the play would be to produce, and points out that it is full of commercial potential ("it has the advantage of being the sort of play that most of the public will appreciate," he writes, tongue firmly in cheek).

Lugné-Poe finally capitulated to Jarry's urbane bludgeoning, although grudgingly. He wasn't convinced that *Ubu Roi* was a masterpiece; rather, he agreed to mount the play because it wouldn't put an undue strain on the Théâtre de l'OEuvre's skimpy budget. Jarry also had an ally in the ever-devoted Rachilde, who had been Lugné-Poe's friend and patron for a number of years, and who wrote him a letter urging him not only to stage *Ubu*, but to allow Jarry a free hand in the production of the play. With these two persuasive voices at his ear, Lugné-Poe's resistance was eventually beaten down, but as we shall see, he was ultimately to prove a fair weather friend both to *Ubu Roi* and to forward-looking drama as well.

Once *Ubu Roi* was firmly entrenched in the schedule for the upcoming season, Jarry threw himself headlong into the promotion of his monstrous brainchild. He utilized his artistic abilities to plaster Paris with flyers, posters, and grandiose announcements; he deluged the art publications with woodcuts of Pa Ubu. Lugné-Poe, alarmed at these visions of Ubu in the flesh, almost backed out at the last minute, but in true vaudeville fashion, the show went on.

On the night of the premiere, December 11, 1896, the Théâtre Nouveau in the Rue Blanche was overflowing with intellectuals of all stripes—the brightest minds of Paris had all turned out to see Jarry's debut as a dramatist. No one had any idea what to expect; it is a safe bet that there wasn't anyone in the audience who was prepared for what was to follow.

Despite the fact that the audience was already restless, the curtain remained down and a makeshift table was brought out and placed in front of it. Then Jarry himself appeared, walking like an android, and sat down stiffly on a chair behind the table. Attired in a baggy black suit, his hair "plastered down like Bonaparte," this pale-faced apparition addressed the audience for about ten minutes. His speech was even more metallic and mechanical than usual, and he gulped nervously from a glass of water at his elbow. First he thanked the critics who had praised *Ubu Roi* when it had been published, then he proceeded to warn in an oblique and ironic way that the character of Ubu was both more and less than what it seemed. "You are free to see in M. Ubu as many allusions as you like, or if you prefer, just a plain puppet, a schoolboy's caricature of one of his teachers who represented for him everything in the world that is grotesque," he intoned. Next he went on to explain that the entire production had been "put on in some haste and in a spirit of friendly improvisation"—there had been no time to construct a mask for Ubu, for instance; cuts had been made in the script, perhaps to its detriment, while other scenes had been left in which Jarry would "have been only too happy to eliminate"; and, Jarry admitted, he and his celebrated scene-painters (which included Toulouse-Lautrec, Sérusier, and Bonnard) had "been up all night" painting last-minute props. He apologized for the reduction of the grand orchestra originally planned to accompany *Ubu*, which had shrunk from a Wagnerian aggregation heavy on the timpani and trombones—"to cover up the catcalls," he had written—to "a few drums and pianos executing *Ubu*'s themes." (Actually, the orchestra consisted of one piano played four-hands by

Claude Terrasse, who had composed the original music for the play, and his wife. Terrasse also jumped up from time to time to slam a pair of cymbals together.)

Finally Jarry wound up his speech: "And the action, which is about to start, takes place in Poland—that is to say, Nowhere." (Poland, as a result of partition and political chaos, was in 1896 virtually absent from the map.) Then Jarry rose, picked up his table, and exited. The overture began and the curtain inched its way up.

The audience had been loud and restless during Jarry's speech, but they calmed down a little as the magnificent actor Fermin Gémier, on loan from the Comédie Francaise, strode to center stage. He cut a bloated and grotesque figure in a padded, pear-shaped costume with concentric circles ringing an enormous belly. Beside him was his female counterpart, Louise France, in an equally bizarre get-up, looking like a depraved Judy in a Punch-and-Judy show. These horrendous characters were Pa and Ma Ubu, a demented duo personifying the basest proclivities of the human race, simultaneously fatuous and bloodthirsty, banal and brutal—a 19th-century Ozzie and Harriet about to embark on an unthinkable spree of crime which had no peer in the annals of drama.

And now Gémier bellowed a single word in a voice that was brazen and mechanical like Jarry's own, but far more horrifying: "*MERDRE*!" (That is, "shitr.")

He was unable to get a word in edgewise for the next fifteen minutes. Never in modern drama had anyone used such language—and Jarry had compounded the felony by adding the extra "r" in order to make sure no one missed the obscenity! Of course no one did. A number of faint-hearted auditors fled, shrieking, up the aisles of the theatre. A *mêlée* broke out in the orchestra pit, punctuated by flailing limbs and threatening fists. In the front rows, Jarry's numerous supporters yelled, "You wouldn't have understood Shakespeare or Wagner, either!" while in answer Jarry's opponents, equally numerous, repeated the word they had just heard hurled at them from the stage. Some members of the audience were so confused that they applauded approvingly and whistled derisively at the same time. Everyone, regardless of opinion, turned in their seats and craned their necks to see the reaction of the drama critics who had turned out in full force and were now most assuredly on the hot seat. A goodly number of these appeared as though they didn't know whether to shitr or go blind. They were undoubtedly wishing that they were somewhere else, viewing a nice safe evening of Racine.

At last Gémier, despairing of ever being able to continue, improvised a jig and threw himself across the prompter's box, managing at last to call

the raging house to order. Then he proceeded with the play's next line—
another "*Merdre!*" Once again, pandemonium reigned supreme. Howls
of protest and of approbation rose to the very ceiling of the Théâtre
Nouveau. There would be nothing comparable to this public madness until, perhaps, the premiere of Stravinsky's "Le Sacre du Printemps" in
1913. Eventually, however, Gémier was able to quiet the raging
multitudes enough to get on with the business at hand—which consisted
of murdering, pillaging, seizing power by brute force, loitering with
intent—in short, smearing shitr on everything in sight.

Never before had any play taken such a dim view of humanity. Its plot
is simple, a skeleton lifted from Shakespeare and Chabrier, filtered
through the jaundiced eye of Lautrèamont. By treachery and intrigue (and
goaded on by the equally greedy Ma Ubu), the rapacious Pa Ubu manages
to murder the King of Poland. After taking the king's place on the throne,
Pa Ubu immediately does away with such niceties as due process of law;
he also insists that his subjects must deliver up all their worldly goods,
or be slaughtered. However, the wealth of Poland is not enough to satisfy
him. Urged on by Ma Ubu (who has designs on the wealth of Poland
herself), Ubu declares war on Russia, but when he discovers that there is
more to warfare than he had bargained for, he deserts. Meanwhile, in his
absence Ma Ubu attempts to rob the royal crypt, but her plan is foiled and
she is forced to flee a raging mob. She is finally reunited with Pa Ubu in
a cavern in the mountains, where he has gone to hide from the Russians
and from the Poles as well. In the play's final scene, the Ubus are seen

sailing blithely back to France, where they will no doubt repeat their Polish performance.

In its all-pervasive desire to pound human morality to a bloody pulp, *Ubu Roi* not only served as an extremely grotesque and unflattering funhouse mirror to the ignobility of the human condition, but it also created an entirely new category of drama—that of absurdism. On that evening in 1896 the Theater of the Absurd was born, ushering in a whole new age of philosophical irrationality. Many others would subsequently explore this territory—in fact, the Theater of the Absurd would, through the works of dramatists such as Beckett and Ionesco, become accepted as part of the mainstream of 20th-century drama—but no one would ever be able to match Jarry's ferocity or inventiveness in exposing the fundamental horror underlying the mundane. Ubu was the first (and by virtue of his primacy the most horrifying) inhuman protagonist in drama, the dramatic harbinger of our own senseless and angst-ridden epoch. His evil was all the more incomprehensible because it had no positive side to counterbalance it, for Ubu was not meant to be an individual; rather, he was intended by Jarry to represent a thoroughly evil Antichrist. (Jarry had attacked the bourgeoisie squarely on their home front—that of religion.) It is important to note that Ubu's horrible deeds are never stopped or even questioned; nor is he ever punished for any of his crimes. The point is that Ubu is supreme, and that in Jarry's conception of the universe there is no entity greater than Ubu.

Jarry's view of human nature as thoroughly base, and the universe as a foul hell-hole where evil always triumphs, was understandably horrifying to many of those who were exposed to it for the first time. But despite the violence and horror of *Ubu Roi*, there was also a transcendent humor which was missed by the less perceptive—the ironic humor of someone who was enough of a megalomaniac to sit back and view the entire human condition as a demented puppet theater. In fact, Jarry had originally intended his play to be performed by marionettes, with himself pulling the strings. At the premiere of *Ubu Roi*, he no doubt found it extremely amusing to be able to yank on the strings of the various members of the audience and get them to roar with approval or howl with disgust. For a twenty-three-year-old midget from Laval—that is to say, Nowhere—that was no mean feat. And *Ubu Roi* remains able to elicit that sort of powerful reaction from audiences today. It is a play which is timeless in its ability to elicit the most profound, visceral responses— horror, bewilderment, the total experience of the purely absurd—from its audiences, and as such, whatever its pros and cons, it is a work of genius. Before *Ubu*, the absurdist category didn't even exist; afterward, not only did the artistic philosophy begin to accept the notion that the human condition was ridiculous, but also the fact that this absurd tragedy could be accepted with equanimity and even humor.

At Home With Pa Ubu

There were only two performances of *Ubu Roi* at the Théâtre Nouveau, and then the curtain rang down on Jarry's perverse masterpiece of hatchetry and nihilism, not to rise again until 1908, the year after his death. But those two performances were enough to set the entire Parisian literary world ablaze with arguments, counter arguments, rationales, attacks, defenses, and dismissals—everyone, it seemed, had something to say about Pa Ubu. The biggest bone of contention was whether Jarry, with a single blow, had liberated drama from outmoded strictures and enabled it to take any sort of direction it wished in the future, or if he had merely obliterated conventional dramatic forms with brutal mindlessness, failing to replace them with anything significant. In other words, it was the classic controversy which inevitably surrounds the emergence of a new art form.

The drama critics of Paris fell on Jarry's play with almost Ubuesque zeal, snarling and gnawing away at one another as well as at the bone of contention. The battle between pro and con was typified by two important members of the critical ranks—Henry Bauer of the *Echo de Paris*, a good friend of Jarry's who, along with Catulle Mendès and a number of others, represented the more forward-looking group that supported Jarry and *Ubu*; and Henry Fouquier of *Le Figaro*, who, although he was sympathetic to avant-garde literature, had no love for *Ubu Roi*. Yet even Fouquier was obliged to admit that Jarry's monstrous play "brought a kind of release . . . At least it has begun to put an end to the Terror which has been reigning over our literature." However, Bauer summed up the magnitude of *Ubu*'s impact the more succinctly: "From this huge and strangely suggestive figure of Ubu blows the wind of destruction, of inspiration for contemporary young people, which overthrows the traditional respects and scholarly preconceptions. And the type will remain."

Jarry himself appeared unconcerned with the raging *Ubu* debate, but one development in the controversy was to affect him extremely adversely, nipping his embryonic career as a playwright in the bud before he could even begin to cash in on his new-found notoriety. Largely as a result of the critical controversy surrounding *Ubu Roi*, Lugné-Poe, never a staunch supporter of Jarry or his artistic philosophy, completely abandoned his avant-garde approach to theater, and even the staging of plays by French playwrights! It was a serious blow for Jarry, for the Théâtre de l'OEuvre had been the most progressive drama group in Paris, and when it retrenched there was no other theater troupe daring enough to produce his work. But nonetheless, Pa Ubu's checkered career was just beginning. That bombastic and overwhelming character was about to begin his domination of his creator's plays, prose, verse, and—to a certain extent—even Jarry himself.

There is no doubt that Jarry's public behavior was every bit as exaggerated and cartoonish as his writing. In that dense crowd of crazed and flamboyant Parisian literary *paroxystes*, Jarry was the most extreme, the most outré—and the most-copied. All of this was extremely appropriate for a man whose self-described passion was *"les BizArts,"* and it not only camouflaged his unprepossessing origins, but it also won him the respect of his fellow artists as well.

Roger Shattuck, whose landmark biographical essay on Jarry in the book *The Banquet Years* served to introduce a whole new generation of readers to Jarry and his work, observed that a biography of Jarry invariably ends by being about someone else. Shattuck claimed that Jarry ultimately annihilated his real personality and became a law unto himself, a truly original creation which required new, almost non-human, methods of interpretation to be fully understood. This theory, while certainly intriguing, fails to take a number of factors into account, and worse yet, tends to obscure the human side of Jarry, and the inner conflicts which ultimately forged his personality. In trying to come to terms with Jarry's bizarre behavior it is important to remember that just beneath the surface of his ongoing one-man sideshow was a human being in a state of profound psychological, intellectual, and spiritual anguish. The separation of his parents, Mme. Jarry's eccentric behavior, the ridicule of the Laval villagers, Jarry's divided loyalties to France and to Brittany, his self-consciousness about his short stature, and perhaps most importantly, his love-hate relationhip with the Catholic church—all played a part in the creation of his subsequent persona. Moreover, Jarry was first and foremost a product of a society in a state of advanced decay—his own troubled childhood bore that out—so it was little wonder that the specter of Ubu, the supreme axe-wielder, became such an obsession for him. His bizarre personification of Ubu was a way of making a statement about himself and the conditions around him; by transforming himself into a public facsimile of Ubu, he could both camouflage his own inauspicious origins and comment on the Ubuness he saw everywhere. His chief interest was always in escaping from the mundane, and like everything else he did, he did it with ferocious thoroughness. In the process, he also came exhilaratingly close to closing the gap between life and art, obsession and action, "reality" and "unreality," thus causing many observers to confuse his life with his art.

The danger of speculating about Jarry's inner motivations, of course, lies in the fact that the nature of his life lent itself to much misinterpretation and distortion by his contemporaries, especially by later writers who did not know him. The urge to create a fictional, symbolic character from Jarry's exploits is at times overpowering. He himself made matters worse by acting, in essence, as his own P.T. Barnum; sometimes, after pulling off some flamboyant stunt or other, he would ask the question, "But isn't it lovely as literature?" Step right up, ladies and gentlemen, and see the midget from Laval transformed into the Supermale of the Ages right before your very eyes! The paradoxical desire to attract attention to himself without revealing any part of his true personality was one which he had possessed since early childhood; and through this motivation he attempted to fuse life and literature in one unbroken act, rendering the whole greater than its parts while meanwhile diverting attention away from the fact that he was, after all, hardly the Supermale of the Ages. Thus, since his was basically a philosophically alienated nature, he accordingly presented the cartoon of an alienated persona to the world.

His one-man sideshow was extremely elaborate and all-encompassing; he changed everything in his life to conform to it. In doing so, his chief concern seemed to be that the sheer inappropriateness of his actions should reveal his fundamental disgust with the absurdity of life. To begin with, there was his attire. He often dressed in a bicycle racer's costume, with his pants legs stuffed into his socks and a pair of "holy"-toed canvas shoes on his feet; but he sometimes donned the sweeping black cape and tall silk hat he had worn at the Lycée Henri IV. Of course, he wore the bicycling outfit to fancy literary *soirees*, and the cape and hat on random peregrinations around town. One night he and a friend went to hear a light opera, courtesy of the opera's composer, who knew them both and had supplied them with complimentary passes. Jarry came attired in a grubby white canvas suit with a homemade paper shirt underneath; he had painted a smeary tie on the front of the shirt, using India ink. His friend wore a fur cap and brandished a shepherd's crook. Because the two would-be operagoers did not live up to the acceptable dress code, the manager of the opera house exiled them to a back balcony. Nonplussed, Jarry waited until the curtain was going up and then announced in a loud, abrasive monotone, audible to everybody in the theater: "I don't see why they allow the audience in the first three rows to come in carrying musical instruments."

Being small enough to fit into it, Jarry also wore women's clothing, claiming that it was less confining than men's garments. On the occasion of Mallarmé's funeral, he borrowed Rachilde's fanciest yellow shoes.

He considered firearms to be an extension of his wardrobe and never went anywhere without a few miscellaneous weapons distributed about his person, frequently walking the streets of Paris at night with a carbine slung over his shoulder and two pistols stuck into his belt. One night a passerby with a cigarette walked up to him and asked for a light. "*Voilà*," Jarry replied with impeccable politeness, and blazed away with his revolver in the direction of the unfortunate fellow's cigarette. The youthful Pablo Picasso was so impressed by Jarry's finesse with weapons that he began aping him by carrying around an equal number of firearms. (Later, he would paint Jarry's portrait and amass a valuable collection of original Jarry man-

uscripts, as well as acknowledging Jarry's influence on his Cubist period.)

In 1897 Jarry, along with Vallette, Rachilde, and several other writers, rented a rambling house in Corbeil, on the Seine—a retreat Jarry dubbed "The Phalanstery." There, Jarry was often to be found with his pistols, plugging away at various targets in the backyard; he practiced so often, in fact, that he began laying in hundred-pound barrels of gunpowder. He had the deplorable habit, according to Rachilde, of taking blind potshots at the trees on the other side of the wall that separated the Phalanstery from the houses of its more sedate neighbors. One afternoon the mistress of the house next door came flying to Rachilde in a panic, claiming that Jarry's pataphysical pistol practice was surely going to kill one or more of her children, who played in the yard. Jarry himself was standing nearby, and when he overheard this conversation he remarked regally, "If that evil hour ever arrives, Ma-da-me, we will be happy to make some others with you."

When it came to the matter of food and especially of drink, Jarry was clearly in a class by himself, as usual. He was an amazing fisherman who could catch fish anywhere in the Seine, using an improvised fishing line. (There would come a point toward the end of his life when his fishing line would be the only buffer between him and starvation.) He even trans-planted his fishing skills to land, learning to fish with deadly accuracy from a tree for the chickens roosting in the yard of the Phalanstery's long-suffering next door neighbors.

Jarry soon became known as an unholy terror to the waiters of the restaurants he patronized. To demonstrate his hatred of bourgeois convention, he ordered his meals backwards and even inside-out, sometimes reversing the courses so that he started with dessert and finished with soup, other times mangling the order of the courses with no rhyme or reason. But where Jarry really stood out as a man apart from the mob was in his consumption of alcohol. Among the literary and artistic types of Paris, excessive drinking was, of course, taken for granted; wine (especially of the cheap red variety) flowed like water, and harder stuff was also routinely imbibed to lend punch to mystico-poetical musings. Jarry, however, went far beyond the excesses engaged in by his fellow debauchees; his daily intake, as recorded with awe and horror by Rachilde, went as follows:

> As an eye-opener, first thing upon arising, two liters of white wine.
> Between 10:00 A.M. and noon, three shots of absinthe.
> With lunch, red or white wine, followed by still more absinthe.
> In the afternoon, several cups of coffee with plenty of marc brandy to wash it down with.
> During and after dinner, various *apéritifs*. Also a couple more bottles of wine.

Absinthe was Jarry's drink of choice (perhaps because, as we all know, it makes the heart grow fonder), although Rachilde points out that when he was short of funds, which was often the case, he would substitute cheap wine or ether. (In his writing, he always referred to the most exalted mental plane as "ethernity.") Once, when he was dying of thirst and there wasn't enough absinthe for a good gulp, Jarry got to experimenting around in his own inimitable fashion and came up with a mixture that would undoubtedly have gladdened the heart of my estimable collaborator Bill Griffith's comic strip character, Zippy the Pinhead: a glassful of absinthe, vinegar, and ink. *A votre santé!*

As might be expected, Jarry's assessment of teetotallers was incisive. "Anti-alcoholics," he observed scornfully, "are unfortunates in the grip of water, that terrible poison, so solvent and corrosive that out of all substances it has been chosen for washings and scourings." Furthermore, he explained with distaste, "a drop of water, added to a clear liquid like absinthe, muddies it." Nasty stuff, that H_2O.

Jarry's surreal elbow-bending soon passed beyond the point of legend and into the realm of archetype. His hometown of Laval was known for producing a staggering number of alcoholics (or should that be a number of staggering alcoholics?), and like a true Lavalois, Jarry regarded alcohol as the water of life. He viewed it as a skeleton key that allowed him to enter into the realms of the dream state, an elevated plane of existence where the commonplace could not penetrate and exceptionality was the rule. Alcohol was his last refuge against the savage onslaught of reality: when further physical transformation of the insipid and mediocre became impossible, he turned to drink.

The nature of Jarry's various living quarters may also have had something to do with his drinking. With one exception, they tended to be dank, decadent, and depressing—although for all we know, Jarry may have found them cheerful. In 1895, when his father Anselme died of influenza in Laval—"right on schedule," Alfred noted sourly—he left his son the family home in Laval as well as a small inheritance. Jarry immediately gave up the "Dead Man's Calvary," where he himself had nearly died of influenza, and moved into far fancier quarters on the Boulevard Saint-Germain. Here he installed a marionette theater with which to amuse visitors. He also whiled away the hours bouncing dried peas off the hats of the gentlemen walking by in the street below. However, such splendor did not last long; between the rent on these palatial quarters and the founding of a lavish graphic magazine, *Perhinderion* (the name of which meant "pilgrimage" in Breton), devoted to printing the engravings of Albrecht Dürer plate by plate, Jarry had soon eaten up his inheritance. His next lodgings were located in a cramped little cubicle located on the second-and-a-half floor of an old building at number 7, rue Cassette. To this reduction of an apartment he gave the grand name of "Our Grand Chasublerie," because the first floor of the building housed an ecclesiastical smock-hawker. The rapacious owner of 7, rue Cassette had decided that since the ceilings of his building were extremely high, he could get twice as many apartments by splitting the existing flats in half horizontally.

The Grand Chasublerie remained Jarry's principal residence for the rest of his life, even though (or perhaps because) his head rubbed against the ceiling when he stood up, and his visitors were obliged to stay crouched on the floor. Jarry had almost no furniture; and what he did have was—like everything else about the Grand Chasublerie—a "reduction" of one kind or another. This included Jarry's desk (he wrote lying on his stomach on the floor), his library (a single edition of Rabelais plus a few other books), and Jarry's portrait by Rousseau (which Jarry had hacked away at until only the head was left). Adorned in a velvet skullcap, an enormous stone phallus stood solemnly on the mantel. One day a lady visitor, spying this member for the first time, had blushingly asked, "Is that a cast?"

"No," Jarry had answered without missing a beat. "It is a re-duc-tion."

Jarry's pompous style of speech soon came to be known as "*le parler Ubu*" among the Parisian literati, who outdid one another in attempting to copy it. But "Ubuspeak" remained the sole property of its originator, whose metallic, unaccented delivery was both mechanical and manic. Never breaking character, Jarry's everyday speech was marked by the use of the royal "we" and by an idiosyncratic tendency to refer to things and people as "that which"; the wind was "that which blows," his bicycle was "that which rolls," and an express train became, in a characteristic pun, "that which drags" (*tráine*). According to Rachilde, this often made normal conversation with Jarry difficult, as might be imagined.

Given the nature of things, however, sooner or later Jarry was bound to encounter obstacles in his transformation of objective reality into his own intellectual amusement park. At that point Pataphysics was born—Jarry's pseudo-scientific system which provided him with a way to limit the amount of noxious mediocrity that seeped into his otherwise exceptional world.

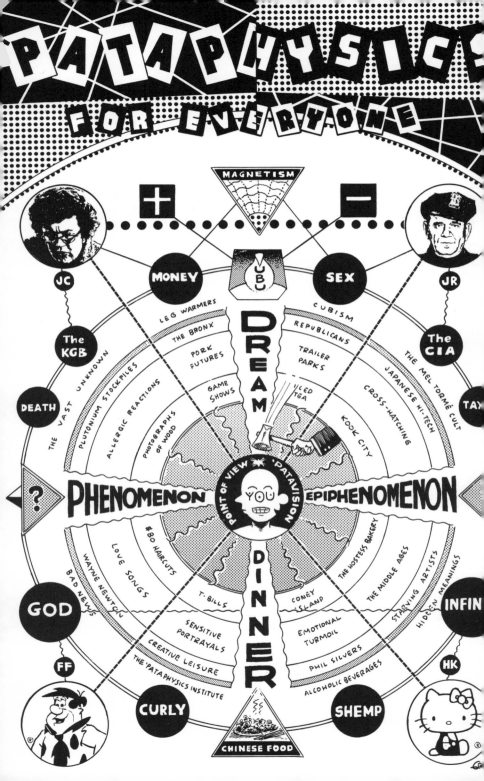

What Is Pataphysics? or Turkistan Revisited

First of all, let us begin by ruling out what Pataphysics is not. It is heartening to commence with such a simple and easy task, for when it comes to the precise and accurate dissection of matters pataphysical, many are called but few are chosen.

1. Pataphysics is not an expensive and demanding socio-psychological regime. One need not attend interminable pataphysical meetings where one is not allowed to use the sanitary facilities for hours on end. In fact, one cannot attend such meetings with a pataphysically good conscience; they cannot exist and still be considered truly pataphysical.

2. Pataphysics is not the pet theory of a small group of crackpots who distribute badly photocopied pamphlets trumpeting their obsession from a post office box in Glendale, California.

3. Pataphysics is not likely to become the next dance craze. It hasn't got a beat and you can't dance to it.

4. Pataphysics is not to be found as a subject heading in the Subject Headings List of the Library of Congress. Therefore, it must not exist.

Although the measured and archaic syllables of its designation make it sound Latin or Greek, Pataphysics is neither. Rather, Pataphysics was born when the immense and rapacious belly, or horngut (*cornegidouille*) of Pa Ubu was transmuted by a single stroke (*patte à physique*) into a pure and noble science. This is why Pataphysics is often written 'Pataphysics —the apostrophe serves to prevent a distressing pun (*patte à physique*, meaning to pat the belly) and also to indicate the magnitude of the transformation from plus to minus, positive to negative, Ubu to ethernity.

Pataphysics represents Jarry's personal system of phenomenological explanation, a sort of rationale for the absurdity inherent in the universe. He claimed that it extends as far beyond metaphysics as metaphysics extends beyond ordinary physics—in either direction. (The term "quantum metaphysics" comes to mind, but we will let it pass.) Pataphysics is dedicated to examining the laws which govern exceptions, which is why there is no such thing as a true pataphysical organization. By their very nature, organizations are formulated on the shepherd-and-the-flock theory; there cannot be any such thing as a genuine individual in a milling flock of sheep, and even the shepherd is taking his orders from somebody else. Thus, if you should ever see a large group of people renting an auditorium somewhere and claiming to be the First World Congress of Pataphysicians, you would be correct in assuming that they were not pataphysicians at all, but rather sheep posing as pataphysicians.

Pataphysics is devoted to the study of the *epiphenomenon*, or that which is superimposed upon the phenomenon, usually by accident. Furthermore, Jarry explains: "*'Pataphysics is the science of imaginary solutions, which symbolically attributes the properties of objects, described by their virtuality, to their lineaments.* The actual science is based on the principle of induction: the majority of men have seen most often a particular phenomenon preceded or followed by another, and conclude that it will always be like that. But this is only the most frequent case because of one's viewpoint, and it is codified according to convenience."

Not surprisingly, the single best definition of pataphysical postulates remains Jarry's own life—a singularly epiphenomenal occurrence. From the standpoint of cursory observation, Jarry's life seems so absurd and alienated as to be virtually meaningless, but Pataphysics accepts no one point of view as final, preferring that the individual himself be the final judge of the matter. In that sense, Jarry's life can thus be seen as the pataphysical symphony it was. Pataphysics was many things to Jarry—an antidote to religious foolishness; a way of obliging the maddeningly divergent vagaries of life to fit neatly within the limitless confines of an all-purpose construct; a method of synthesis under which nothing was incompatible with anything else.

Pataphysics concentrates on the unification of opposites; as Jarry himself observed, "Between the left side and the right, there is one direction: above." In one of his comic strips my noteworthy colleague Bill Griffith has theorized on the ability of humor to unify opposites and by extension to transcend the limitations of the ordinary; during the brief instant when the humor of a particular perplexing situation causes us to laugh, he observes, we are able to escape the mechanical strictures of ordinary thought and penetrate the limitless realm of the infinite. This was undoubtedly Jarry's intention with Pataphysics. He attempted to live in the realm of ethernity as much as possible by transforming every facet of himself and his environment that he possibly could, and by knocking

down the barriers between conscious and subconscious with alcohol and ether, interjecting the dream state into the waking state. When further expansion into ethernity became impossible, when alcohol and even ether failed to liberate him from the sheer mediocrity of ordinary consciousness, he turned to, or rather invented, Pataphysics. And thus he left us a testament to the inherent resourcefulness of the human intellect as well as a road map into the exhilarating realms of the previously unknown and ostensibly unknowable.

The book in which Jarry explains Pataphysics is *Exploits and Opinions of Doctor Faustroll, Pataphysician*. Following the world premiere of *Ubu Roi* in 1896 and Lugné-Poe's alarmingly conservative reaction to it, Jarry was more or less obliged to put his dramatic interests on the back burner. Instead of continuing to write for the stage, he turned to novels, essays, and poetry. His most important and significant project during this period was the completion of *Faustroll*.

Subtitled *A Neo-Scientific Novel*, *Faustroll* is nothing if not pataphysical. It veers back and forth between the exalted world of scientific speculation of H. G. Wells or Jules Verne, and the good-natured vulgarity of Rabelais. The name of the novel's protagonist, Doctor Faustroll, is a compound of "Faust" and "troll," typifing Jarry's view of the duality inherent in mankind. (Jarry was fond of the works of Henrik Ibsen and had supervised the staging of Ibsen's *Peer Gynt* at the Théâtre de l'Oeuvre, in which he played the part of a troll.) Human beings, he seems to be saying in *Faustroll*, are base creatures (which accounts for the "troll" element), but like Faust, we are nevertheless driven to seek after higher truths even if such a search ultimately means our destruction.

The novel records the voyage of Faustroll and an unlikely entourage of two "from Paris to Paris" in a boat which is a sieve. His companions on this voyage are Rene-Isidore Panmuphle (or "All-Snout"), a bailiff who is dunning him for the sum of "Three Hundred and Seventy-two thousand francs 27 centimes, in respect of Eleven quarters rental" on a flat in Paris; and Bosse-de-Nage (in the pseudo-archaic French Jarry loved to affect, literally "Ass-Face," or more politely "Hump-O-Rump"), a "dog-faced baboon less cyno- than hydrocephalous, and, as a result of this blemish, less intelligent than his fellows." Bosse-de-Nage's vocabulary is generally limited to two words—"Ha ha!"—with which he greets Faustroll's profound observations throughout the voyage. The brilliant red and blue patches on his posterior have been transposed by Faustroll to the baboon's cheeks, so that his face resembles a tricolor (hail France!), and this brilliant coloration serves to supply the travelers with a source of light as they sail along the streets of Paris by night in their odd vessel.

Jarry got the idea for Faustroll's skiff from reading about the experiments of the British scientist Charles Vernon Boys, whose area of research was the surface tension of soap bubbles. The skiff is constructed of mesh fabric which is coated with melted paraffin; placed in water, the "skin" of the water tightens against the holes of the mesh, so that the water below the skiff cannot penetrate the skiff's surface unless the water's "skin" is itself somehow punctured. Luckily, however, the skiff is not subjected to water, but is instead propelled through the streets of Paris by suction disks at the end of spring levers, while the boat's keel is

supported by three steel rollers. Thus Jarry was able to avoid the very unpataphysical and distressingly prosaic dilemma of whether or not Faustroll's vessel would actually be seaworthy.

Sailing through the streets of Paris in the skiff, Faustroll and his companions stop to visit many of the members of the Parisian intellectual world. Each chapter of *Faustroll* carries a dedication to one of Jarry's friends or foes in the arts, and each gives Jarry's impression of that person and his work. One of the reasons *Faustroll* holds our interest today is because it represents a turn-of-the-century Parisian "Who's Who" of the arts, an inventive way for Jarry to pay homage to the friends he loved and castigate the foes he hated. It also shows the depth of his affection for his friends, as well as his extreme sensitivity and intelligence in perceiving the various natures of their artistic contributions. In viewing Jarry as a mechanized mutant midget it is all too easy to forget that he possessed some sterling virtues, the chief of which was loyalty to his friends.

After Faustroll and company complete their voyage from Paris to Paris by sieve, the novel becomes even more pataphysical. Although he has previously dismissed death as "only for the mediocre," Faustroll nonetheless succumbs, and he then proceeds to send "telepathic letters" to the scientist Lord Kelvin (whose experiments with magnetism, electricity, and solar power intrigued Jarry) from the other regions. Using his "posthumous leisure," Faustroll conducts an in-depth study of "ethernity" and dutifully reports his findings to Kelvin: "The sun is a cold, solid, and homogeneous globe. Its surface is divided into squares of one meter, which are the bases of long inverted pyramids . . ."

Finally Faustroll undertakes the ultimate pataphysical experiment: ascertaining the surface of God. After some virtuoso calculations he arrives at the conclusion that "God is the shortest distance between zero and infinity.

"In what direction? one may ask.

" ± We shall reply that His first name is not Jack, but Plus-and-Minus. And one should say:

"God is the shortest distance between 0 and ∞ in either direction.

"Which conforms to the belief in the two principles; but it is more correct to attribute the sign + to that of the subject's faith."

At the end of *Faustroll* is the conclusion:

" 'Pataphysics is the science . . .'"

On the bottom of the last page of the original manuscript of *Faustroll*, Jarry wrote in his large, flowing handwriting the following very curious apostrophe: "This book will not be published integrally until the author has acquired sufficient experience to savor all its beauties in full." Since in the novel Faustroll experiences death and goes on to measure and analyze ethernity, Jarry obviously did not think that the book would be published in his own lifetime. And he was correct; *Faustroll* did not appear in print until 1911, four years after Jarry died.

Thus *Faustroll* comes to an end. Part intellectual flea market, part loving tribute to artistic friends, part pseudo-scientific speculation, and all Pataphysics, it is as good a definition of pataphysical principles as any. Somewhere between "Plus and Minus" lies the actual enumeration of Pataphysics—a circular plane where neither plus nor minus are relevant and everything is equally possible. At one end of the spectrum we see Pa Ubu, indicative of the basest instincts in mankind; at the other end, perhaps, the Supermale, he who "goes beyond everything hitherto imaginable"; and at the center, Faustroll, dipping back and forth between good and evil, negative and positive, weighing and balancing in truly detached scientific fashion. Jarry's life was often troubled and dreary, and he strove mightily to obliterate any traces of the inauspicious origins which might have made him less than exceptional—but through Pataphysics he was able to transform himself from a negligible quantity of atoms into an entity which was important enough to become a law unto itself.

"It's a Female, but a Very Strong One": The Tears of the Supermale

Jarry always claimed that because he had been born on the Feast of the Nativity of the Holy Virgin, he suffered from a pronounced dislike for members of the female sex. No doubt the Freudians would have a grand old time picking through the multitude of early childhood experiences and attendant bizarre psychological kinks that left their imprint on Jarry and made him such a profound misogynist. Chief among these childhood bugaboos was undoubtedly the titanic figure of Caroline Jarry, the eccentric and devoted mother figure of whom, Alfred explained, "we had to approve before we were old enough to have a voice in the matter." He literally owed his lifespring—his education and pronounced individuality—to his mother, who had made a commendable stand for independence by leaving her bourgeois husband and striking out on her own in order to further her son's education. But any parent with that strong a personality is bound to have an adverse affect on a child, and Mme. Jarry's dominating character may have created in her son a fear of women which in time became externalized as scorn and disgust. Throughout Jarry's writing, he portrays women as huntresses, always seeking to entrap unwary males with seeming acquiescence, but when the prey has been drawn into the silken nets of love, destruction speedily follows.

Another cause underlying this attitude was no doubt the Catholic faith into which Jarry had been born and with which he struggled throughout his life. Religion (along with science and sex) was one of Jarry's major concerns as a writer. His childhood and adolescence in the mystical backwater of Brittany had loaded Jarry down with a great deal of theological baggage, and he carried this with him throughout his life, dropping pieces here and there but ultimately reassuming the entire burden in his last years. Although he consciously attempted to replace mysticism with the logical reasoning of scientific speculation, shortly before dying he asked for the last sacraments; he would also begin wearing religious medals the year before he died, knowing that his health was rapidly failing and that he might meet his end at any moment.

Like many other brilliant minds in revolt against Catholicism, Jarry was always in an intellectual and emotional muddle when it came to the subject of love and sex. Much of his best writing was devoted to examining the fascinating theme of the human attitude toward the biological function of sex; his fundamentally logical intellect was capable of probing far beneath the surface of social conventions in sexual relationships, and some of his observations ring surprisingly true even while they may not be particularly comforting to those who believe in the essential goodness of humanity. Jarry, of course, took the exact opposite view— beginning with his juvenile scribblings, he consistently portrayed a cockeyed universe over which a malevolent, irrational Deity rode rough-shod, and of course the humans which populated this hellish place could only be expected to behave in an ignoble manner. (Beginning in his *lycée* years and continuing through his adulthood, one of his favorite authors was the Comte de Lautrèamont, whose sole published work, *Les chants de Maldoror*, were dark-hued, misanthropic prose-poems filled with images of violence and mental and physical torment.)

The root of Jarry's misanthropic philosophy was probably Catholicism, which predicates everything on the doctrine of Original Sin; as a result of perfidious Eve's treachery in the Garden of Eden, humankind was instantly reduced from perfection to baseness, there to remain. Thus both women and the human race are not only fallible, but totally corrupt. If by chance we humans attempt something noble, it will invariably fail because we are bound to regress to our natural vile state sooner or later. This philosophy runs through Jarry's writing from beginning to end.

If we take a peep at Jarry's earliest sexual experiences we can see how this philosophy became reinforced in his mind until it took on the dimensions of a dogma. By his own admission, Jarry's first sexual contacts took place with prostitutes in the brothels of Rennes. This proclivity for paid relations apparently continued when he went to Paris, for at one point his visiting card was found by police in the apartment of a high-class Parisian call girl. But most likely the turning point in his sexual career was his relationship with Madame Berthe de Courrière, which took place when Jarry was first beginning to make his mark in Parisian literary circles as a young man of twenty. At one of the *Mercure de France* salons in the Rue de l'Echaude, Jarry was introduced to de Courrière by his friend and publishing partner Remy de Gourmont. Called ''The Old Dame'' by the salon regulars (although not to her face), at the time when Jarry rather reluctantly made her acquaintance Berthe de Courrière was a frankly lecherous, religiously-inclined woman in her mid-forties with fading looks and a propensity for propositioning priests. Some twenty years earlier she had served as a model for the sculptor Clésinger, and she had also lived with the novelist Huysmans, whom she had inspired to write the novel *La-Bas*. Now she was de Gourmont's mistress, a proud but pitiful specimen of aging vanity.

De Courrière was induced to fix her attentions on Jarry by Jean de Tinan, a practical joker in the *Mercure* group; with diabolical humor de Tinan hinted to the Old Dame that the *Mercure*'s pint-sized *enfant terrible* was secretly carrying a torch for her, but that the poor lad was too young and shy to mention it. True to her reputation for vanity, the Old Dame seized this bait whole and proceeded to write Jarry a sizzling love letter which nearly choked on overblown romantic symbolism, while also suggesting that surely Jarry must need someone to sew buttons on his shirts! Jarry was both horrified and fascinated by her invitation, but their liaison did not last long—perhaps he was put off when he discovered that the Old Dame never washed, preferring to keep her skin in shape by anointing it with a daily coating of vaseline which she purchased from a suburban drugstore. Whatever the reason, Jarry abruptly cut the relationship short, but it had already ended his friendship with de Gourmont,

who had been not only his strongest literary supporter but also his publishing partner in the art review *L'Ymagier*.

Despite its brevity, his relationship with the Old Dame left an indelible mark on him. When, in 1898, his novel *The Visits of Love* was published, it contained a chapter entitled "The Old Dame" which described de Courrière down to the last wrinkle and even included a facsimile of her ridiculous love letter to Jarry! Although much of Jarry's writing can be said to be autobiographical in a general sense, this particular chapter was especially frank—so much so that it took all the machinations of Jarry's powerful friends to keep him out of jail for libel. The Old Dame is drawn as scheming, ambitious, deadly, and ultimately sickening—an aged and bloated serpent stuffed with vain fancies, sharpening her tooth as she lies in wait for her next unsuspecting victim. "It was for us that the Trojans died in order to keep Helen," she rhapsodizes. " . . . Come, our time is near. Come, I will give you time and eternity . . . Come, and you will reign; come, and I will carry you into boundless space . . . Come, and you will be the conqueror."

Whether or not the Old Dame in real life was as horrible as the Old Dame in *The Visits of Love* is almost irrelevant—but she made a profound impression on Jarry, and that impression was highly negative. The Oedipal overtones of their ill-fated liaison are hard to deny; surely a twenty-year-old boy is going to feel uncomfortable making love to a woman old enough to be his mother. At any rate, Berthe de Courrière turned out to be his first and last fling—unless, of course, you count Rachilde, with whom he remained on a friendly (and possibly even an intimate) basis until he died. But Rachilde was in an altogether different class than the Old Dame. She was an artist in her own right, a successful author who, while Jarry did not particularly respect her work, he did come to respect as a human being. Rachilde did not employ the standard feminine wiles to gain Jarry's affection; their friendship was based more on the freedom of intellectual interests and acquaintances they had in common rather than

the obligations and limits of conventional romance. Nonetheless, Rachilde's descriptions of Jarry in her biography, *The Supermale of Letters*, betray more than a little lust; she was obviously very attracted to him. As for Jarry, he grants her the (for him) unthinkable favor of including her among the other artists, all otherwise male, whom he mentions in *Doctor Faustroll*. Knowing his "disdain for women, especially women of letters," this is quite a tribute to "Ma-da-me Rachilde" even if it is every bit as left-handed a compliment as "But we will grant you one quality: you do not cling."

Jarry attempted to come to terms with his tangled obsessions of sex, religion, and science in his novel *The Supermale* (*Le surmâle*), which was published in 1902. This novel is set "in the future"—the 1920's—and is an account of André Marcueil, a superman in every sense of the word. Marcueil, although he is far superior to everyone else, feels that he must disguise his superiority from the prying eyes of the world by pretending to be thoroughly average and mundane, a man who "embodied so absolutely the average man that his very ordinariness became extraordinary."

Marcueil sets out to prove that "the act of love is of no importance, since it can be performed indefinitely." This pungent paradox obviously tickled Jarry, and it may have titillated him as well, since in the course of the novel he manages to compose some very passable, if marginal, erotica—restrained, of course, by his characteristically ironic viewpoint, which laughs at the image of human beings as helpless sexual machines driven by libidinous impulses in much the same way as motors are driven by belts and pulleys.

As in many of Jarry's other writings, there are plenty of autobiographical elements in *The Supermale*, although as usual they are scrambled and turned inside out in the same way he altered much else in his life. But thus André Marcueil as a youth strives to remain "pure—if the Catholic faith is correct in terming purity the neglect, under pain of eternal suffering, of certain parts of the body." He soon discovers, however, that despite "trying to exhaust himself by physical exercise," binding himself with thongs, and sleeping on his stomach, he cannot deny that he is not only supremely well-endowed, but also more lustful than a hundred "normal" males. Being logical, he even tries "unnatural" vices, "just long enough to learn by experience what a gap lay between his strength and that of the rest of mankind."

So he goes on, in his adulthood, to make some use of his super-endowments by beating the sexual record set by a certain "Indian" under the influence of a native herb which bestowed almost superhuman powers. Marcueil's partner in this marathon is a young American woman named Ellen Elson, the daughter of a well-known inventor. They manage to best the "Indian's" score, and then Ellen insists that they repeat the act of love once more—"for love." But this last act of love kills Ellen—or so Marcueil erroneously assumes—and as she lies beside him, seemingly dead, he finds that—irony of ironies!—he is in love with her.

However, she is not dead, but only sleeping; for women, Jarry seems to be saying, are sexually indestructible. When Ellen goes home to her father, though, claiming to be in love with Marcueil, the senior Elson's reaction is typically bourgeois: Marcueil must marry Ellen—immediately! In order to convince the "machine-like" Supermale to agree to this, the plucky scientist (who predates Tom Swift by some thirty years) attaches Marcueil to a special machine that has been designed to accomplish the impossible—to change Marcueil's precise, logical, and superior mind, and hopefully force him to marry Ellen.

But science proves highly fallible when used to this questionable end, and Marcueil winds up meeting his death in a bizarre electro-mechanical "crucifixion," thus bringing the novel to a close and bringing Jarry's preoccupation with sex, death, science, and ethernity full (pataphysical) circle. To Jarry, sex and death were inextricably linked, whether it was the death of the body or the death of the spirit. He believed that women were essentially soulless and so could not suffer serious injuries from sexual and romantic adventures, but he also believed that they were more than capable of luring *men* to their doom.

A character as complex and as contradictory as Jarry cannot be easily stuffed into any particular pigeonhole, and his sexuality was as complex and contradictory as any other part of him. It is quite possible to find in his various writings (and, some say, in his life as well) almost any sexual aberration you happen to be looking for, from homosexuality to fetishism. Paradoxically, it is equally possible to find moments of pure eroticism, even though Jarry always manages to pull himself back before he threatens to actually become emotional. Emotional outbursts are extremely unpataphysical. They tie the reactor to a single frame of reference. But *The Supermale* shows that, underneath Jarry's cynical and often brusque facade, there was actually a sensitive human being who had been deeply affected by the restraints and superstitions of the Catholic Church, by his early experiences, and in no small measure by the social unrest of his era. The key to his sexual nature can be found in a recurring line (originally from Lautrèamont, where it referred to one of God's hairs left behind after a wild night in a brothel) which crops up periodically in his writing: "Uprooted phallus, don't jump around so!" Surrounded on all sides by socio-sexual decadence, himself the product of a marriage that was a sneering farce on the bourgeois illusion of domestic bliss, his writings about sex reflect the violent social and political revolution of the *fin-de-siecle*. Like André Marcueil, he sought to subdue his sexual nature with multifarious diversions, but unlike the Supermale, Jarry, being only human, was unable to succeed. His frustrations came spewing forth in a torrent of writing, enriching those who can see beneath the cynicism and irony that mask its all-too-human torment.

From Here to Ethernity

After the publication of *The Supermale* in 1902, Jarry had only five more years to live. Unfortunately, those years were destined to be the most miserable of his life, marked by grueling poverty, increased consumption of alcohol and ether, failing health, and (as might be expected under the circumstances) a tapering-off of literary activity. During most of this time his was a squalid, miserable, hand-to-mouth existence.

The only bright spot in this otherwise thoroughly grim death-in-life was the friendship of several up-and-coming young writers like Guillaume Apollinaire and Max Jacob. They quite rightly saw that Jarry, although fallen on hard times, represented the wave of the future in literary matters. These writers respected and admired Jarry, and he showed his appreciation for their attention by using his influence with various publishers and editors to help them bring their ideas before the public.

Much of the writing Jarry produced during this period was in the form of articles, primarily speculative essays, which appeared in magazines such as *La Revue Blanche* and *Le Canard Sauvage*. Because he desperately needed the money, Jarry wrote many such articles, eventually accumulating a stockpile of 162 of them. He hoped to publish the best of the bunch in book form as *The Green Candle, Light on Things of This Time*, but the project failed to jell. This was extremely unfortunate, for Jarry was at his best when ironically dissecting the various commonplace elements of life which we all take for granted. For instance, in one of his essays he examined the subject of postage stamps and mail delivery from a droll, pseudo-anthropological standpoint, theorizing that stamps must be objects of reverence since we kiss them on the back and then, with blind faith, trust them to somehow ensure the safe delivery of our letters to their destinations. It is this deliberately off-center way of viewing the mundane that defines Jarry's genius as a writer. But the mundane and the depressing were about to sink their petty claws into him nonetheless, and this time absinthe, ether, and Pataphysics were not going to rescue him.

It was apparent to Jarry's friends as early as 1900 that his health was beginning to deteriorate. In November 1903, he accepted an invitation from the composer Claude Terrasse to leave Paris and come to Terrasse's estate in Grand-Lemps in order to collaborate on an *opéra bouffe, Pantagruel*. Terrasse had composed the original music for *Ubu Roi* and had worked closely with Jarry on other projects since then, including *Ubu on* the Mound (*Ubu sur la Butte*), a marionette musical version of *Ubu Roi* which had been published to a very lukewarm reception in 1901. As an old friend of Jarry's, Terrasse was extremely concerned with Jarry's diminishing health, and he hoped that by luring the diminutive dipso-maniac away from his unruly life in Paris, he might also be able to reduce Jarry's consumption of inebriants. They collaborated on the *Pantagruel* libretto off and on until early in 1905, but it was never finished and Ter-rasse finally backed out, realizing that it never would be. Jarry, stubborn as ever, continued working on the opera, but even he finally ran out of steam and eventually abandoned it. He did not, of course, abandon his drinking.

In 1904, Jarry managed to scrape together a little money and purchased some land near the Seine at Coudray, south of Paris. He subsequently decided that he wanted to have a "medieval dungeon" constructed on it, but his funds were insufficient. When the structure was completed, in 1905, it turned out to be more of a shack leaning out over the water on four wobbly stilts. With his usual high-handed disregard for absolutes, Jarry named this flimsy abode the "Tripod" on account of its quartet of legs. At least twice a year, the Seine rose above its banks, and the muddy, sewage-tainted water invariably swamped the Tripod. Furthermore, there

were river rats in abundance, and after a regrettable incident in which the starveling rodents made a meal of the tires on his bicycle, Jarry learned that he had to hang his semi-edible possessions from the ceiling if he didn't want to subsidize the rat population of the Seine.

The end of that year brought further ill health to Jarry. In September he ran the risk of losing a number of teeth. He required some extremely painful dental work; and then in November he had another run-in with his old nemesis, influenza. It was a severe case, dragging on throughout the winter, which happened to be unusually harsh. The Tripod was unheated, and Jarry lay on a straw pallet on its damp floor, alternately burning and freezing as his chills and fever vied with the icy weather outside to see which could make him the most miserable.

Because his illness made it impossible for him to write, Jarry's finances became grim indeed. Although he remained very much a Breton in his staunch sense of independence, he was finally forced to swallow his pride and ask for help from his friends. He began eating most of his meals at the home of the Vallettes, and supplementing his diet with whatever fish he could catch in the Seine. Many times only his hook and line kept him from total starvation.

When the spring finally came, an extremely debilitated Jarry returned to Laval, where his sister Charlotte could look after him. Lying in bed in Laval, he began working on a novel, *The Persecuted* (*La dragonne*), with Charlotte's help. (It would be published in 1943, completed by Charlotte.) Shortly after his arrival, he appeared to be recovering and decided to return to Paris, but he soon suffered a severe relapse and had to drag himself back to Laval once more.

This time, even Jarry felt that he must be dying. The fact that he couldn't summon the strength even to get out of bed thoroughly frightened him, and he allowed the veneer of his usual bravado to crack, abandoning the scorn of all religious matters that had characterized his actions throughout his life. He requested that last rites be administered, and at the same time wrote a painful and touching letter to his oldest friend in Paris, Rachilde.

In a photograph taken a few months earlier, Jarry had appeared strangely pale and listless, with the fire gone out of his dark eyes and his complexion as white as death. He had marked this photograph *"Le Père Ubu s'efface"* ("Pa Ubu is rubbed out"). His letter to Rachilde suggests that, gripped by fever, fear, and confusion, he was no longer certain who he was—if indeed he ever had been. The ironic armor which he had dubbed "Pa Ubu," and which had been his protection against years of artistic disappointment and personal unhappiness, was now melting away, bit by bit, revealing a frightened thirty-three-year-old mortal who could no longer shout belligerently that death was only for the mediocre. Now, ironically, he had to admit that the Grim Reaper was able to reach out and snatch away the exalted and original just as easily as the mundane and the mindless—absurdly, in death there was no differentiation whatsoever.

In his letter to Rachilde, his phraseology is fragmented, and he refers to himself both as "Père Ubu" and "I." He explains to Rachilde with a fleeting touch of his old arrogance that he had just been examined by doctors and found "without blemish, either in the liver or in the heart or in the kidneys." Instead, "He is simply run down (a curious end for the man who wrote *Le surmâle*; his furnace is not going to blow up but simply go out). He will quietly stop running, like a tired motor." Jarry tries desperately to summon his old bravado, stating that he is looking forward to whatever comes after death; he is, he says, "full of an insatiable curiosity." With heart-wrenching eloquence he theorizes about his end: "He will fall back a little further in the darkness of time. Just as he used to carry his revolver in his back pocket, he has put a gold chain around his neck, solely because that metal does not oxidize and will last as long as his bones, with medals in which he believes, just in case he should meet any devils. It's all as much fun as going fishing . . . Père Ubu is shaved and has laid out a mauve shirt just by accident . . . He will start out, still consumed with curiosity. He has a feeling that it will be tonight at five . . . If he is wrong he will be ridiculous and that's that. Ghosts were always ridiculous.

"With this Père Ubu, who has earned his rest, is going to sleep. He believes that the brain, during decomposition, continues to function after death, and that its dreams are our Paradise."

However, not long after writing this last testament, Jarry experienced a partial recovery. Sneering at his own weakness for writing such rubbish and for clutching at the hollow comfort of religion on his "deathbed," he decided once again to return to Paris. Before leaving Laval, he sold the Tripod to Charlotte, realizing that its dismal charms were ill-suited as a place where he could husband his feeble health.

In July 1906, he returned to the Grand Chasublerie at 7, rue Cassette and attempted to resume writing. His finances were so shaky that he desperately sought out markets which he would have scorned earlier, when he was the brightest star on the Parisian avant-garde literary horizon. One such market was *Chanteclair*, a commercial pharmaceutical magazine. With his extensive, if idiosyncratic, knowledge of scientific matters and his fluency in Latin, Jarry would have made a credible contributor to such a journal, but the work he was expecting from the magazine failed to materialize.

Hard hit by increasingly unmanageable financial woes, Jarry approached Terrasse and asked to borrow 750 francs so that he could pay his rent and eat more frequently than he had been. Terrasse, however, was obliged to refuse. In despair, Jarry turned to other friends, some of whom helped out. But the constant financial uncertainty ensured that Jarry's health would never mend. Unable to get enough to eat, he stayed for hours on end in his dismal Grand Chasublerie, lying on his crude, makeshift bed and drinking cheap wine or inhaling ether. He saw less and less of his friends and would sometimes speak incoherently when he did see them.

The last few months of Jarry's life were a galloping nightmare of delirium, illness, and poverty. He spent April through July of 1907 in Laval, then returned to Paris; two days after his return, however, he once again went back to Laval. In October a friend, Alexandre Natanson, lent him enough money to cover the rent at the Grand Chasublerie, and Jarry resumed his residence there on October 17. But he was almost a zombie, far too wasted by the ravages of malnutrition and illness to write, or even to hold up his end of a conversation. One afternoon he and a friend sat down in a cafe so that Jarry could write a letter to Charlotte in Laval. When he handed the letter to the friend to look over, it was completely unintelligible due to missing words and phrases and sheer illegibility.

About this time an old friend received a note from Jarry, imploring him to stop by the Grand Chasublerie and cash some money orders which had arrived from Laval for him. "They must be cashed, or I'm done for," he said simply. "I've been in bed five days without being able to go out and get anything. You'll save my life if you come."

It wasn't long after this that Jarry simply dropped out of sight. No one, not even close friends like the Vallettes, heard anything from him for a number of days. Expecting the worst, Vallette and another friend, Dr. Saltas, went to 7, rue Cassette. Rushing up the stairs to the second-and-a-half floor, they pounded on the door of the Grand Chasublerie, but there was no answer. Finally, after long slow minutes had passed, they heard Jarry's voice, sounding hopelessly faint, telling them that he didn't have the strength to open the door. Upon forcing it open, they burst in and found him, in Saltas' words, "at the back of the room, on the floor, unable to get up. Around him were two empty bottles and a third which was a candleholder." A quick glance showed them that Jarry was paralyzed in both legs and had lost control of his bowels and bladder; the room was indescribably filthy.

Vallette and Saltas picked up the small, wasted body of their friend and carried him downstairs to a carriage that was waiting, then raced to the Hôpital de la Charité. Although he kept slipping in and out of consciousness, Jarry nonetheless wanted to know how the hospital bill was going to be paid; he had no money, he protested weakly, and he didn't want to impose on his friends. When they reassured him that everything would be taken care of, he seemed to relax a little.

At the hospital, the examining doctor offered no hope. Jarry's malady was diagnosed as meningitis tuberculosis. But there was an ironic twist to Jarry's fate nonetheless—he had apparently been correct when he had written to Dr. Saltas from Laval not long before, saying that "Père Ubu, as I am called, is dying not of having done too much drinking, but of not having always had enough to eat." His liver and kidneys appeared to be quite unaffected by his prodigious tippling; it was the chronic malnutrition which had weakened his constitution, leading to the inevitable conclusion of his life.

After remaining in the Hôpital de la Charité for several days, Jarry's breathing grew labored, his pulse diminished almost to nothing, and he became delirious, mumbling over and over, "*Je cherche . . . je cherche . . . j'ch'* . . . (I seek, I seek)." Then he experienced a lucid moment, raising himself slightly in his bed and looking around him almost hopefully. His attending physician, Dr. Stephen Chauvet, hurried over and asked him if he wanted anything. "His eyes began to sparkle," recalled Chauvet. "There was something which would be very nice . . . a toothpick." Saltas ran out and bought a box and handed it to Jarry. "He took one between two fingers of his right hand," Saltas wrote afterward. "Pleasure was visible on his face. I had hardly taken several steps to speak to the orderly when the orderly signaled for me to turn around. Jarry was dead."

It was 4:15 P.M. on November 1, 1907—All Saints' Day. Alfred Jarry had been thirty-four years old.

On November 3, Jarry's funeral procession wound its way to Bagneux cemetery in Paris. All of his friends had turned out to pay him homage—the Vallettes, Saltas, Apollinaire, Fermin Gémier, Louise France, Léon-Paul Fargue, Pierre Bonnard, Paul Valèry, Félix Fenéon, Alexandre Natanson, and others.

Following the simple burial, the group followed Jarry's wishes to the letter and proceeded to eat and especially to drink heartily while recounting the exploits and opinions of their friend, the late, great Pa Ubu.

It was a fitting tribute for a man who had refused to accept the boredom and mediocrity of death almost until the end—a lovingly staged perpetuation of the often-garish cartoon of his life and times. But after awhile the members of the group became subdued, then silent. The fresh mound of earth on Alfred Jarry's grave served as a silent but poignant reminder that no matter to what exalted heights we may climb, none of us can really escape from the dictates and limitations of our fundamental selves. In his absurdly brief lifetime, Jarry had created an unsurpassed art from his personal struggles, had fought to remain extraordinary, and had died in a singular fashion. But he had died just the same. It was a sobering finale to an otherwise thoroughly virtuoso performance.

In 1935, twenty-eight years after Jarry's death, a Jarry scholar, Frederick Pottecher, tried to find the brilliant midget's grave in the Laval cemetery, where the body had eventually been removed to lie in the family plot. It was simply nowhere to be found.

Perhaps Jarry rose from the dead and is even now enjoying his "posthumous leisure" in the upper regions of Ethernity.

It would be somehow heartening to think that he escaped mundanity for once and for all and that the cartoon of his life which he worked so hard at presenting to this world is continuing in another one, before a packed house.

For all we know, he might have even decided to visit Los Angeles, which is, after all, a very irrational place . . .

EPILOGUE: Alfred Jarry— First Sublime Humorist of the Apocalypse

We too shall become solemn, fat, and Ubuesque, and shall publish extremely classical books which will probably lead to our becoming mayors of small towns where, when we become academicians, the pinheads constituting the local intelligentsia will present us with Sèvres vases . . . And another bunch of young people will appear, and find us very old-fashioned, and they will write ballads denouncing us, and there is no reason why they shouldn't.

—Alfred Jarry
(alias Pa Ubu)

Horngut! We shall not have succeeded in demolishing everything unless we demolish the ruins as well; but the only way we can see of doing that is to put up a lot of fine, well-designed buildings.

—Pa Ubu
(alias Alfred Jarry)

In 1909, two years after Alfred Jarry's death, the poet and critic Guillaume Apollinaire wrote a long and perceptive magazine article about the father of Ubu and the architect of pataphysics. By that time, Jarry's writing was already beginning to fade into obscurity, so it was fortunate that Apollinaire's tribute, in which he described Jarry as "the last sublime debauchee of the Renaissance," at least partly ensured that Jarry would not be too quickly forgotten.

Apollinaire had remained close to Jarry until Jarry's death, and he continued to champion the pataphysical cause long afterward. When the Surrealists, led by Apollinaire and André Breton, set up shop in Paris in the late 'teens, they immediately claimed Jarry as their spiritual progenitor. They praised him in their early manifestoes for his experiments with the dream state in literature as well as for his steadfast refusal to ban disturbing or disgusting images from his work. These concrete manifestations of the unconscious mind were to be the hallmarks of the surrealist style, and the early Surrealists were correct in hailing Jarry as the discoverer of their fundamental concepts.

Jarry's influence on the arts in general continued to be felt after "the war to end all wars" cast its irrational shadow on the new century, making his ideas seem less extreme. In 1927, Antonin Artaud founded the Théâtre Alfred Jarry in Paris, vowing to "contribute by strictly theatrical means to the ruin of the theater as it exists today in France," and citing the absurdist humor of *Ubu Roi* as its forerunner and guide in such activities. Artaud's theatrical ideology included the use of film, then a fairly new medium and one which Jarry, with his fascination with the mechanistic and the superhuman, would no doubt have appreciated.

After World War II, English translations of Jarry's writing began slowly to appear; perhaps the figure of Hitler had lent a new and infinitely more disturbing meaning to Ubu's fundamentally mediocre viciousness. Then a spate of American and English *Ubu* productions appeared during the rugged-individualist 1950s, followed by a series of articles on Jarry and some of his contemporaries in the *Evergreen Review*. This was, of course, a time when existential philosophy was all the rage among disenchanted postwar intellectuals, and the existentialists discovered that Jarry's pataphysical musings were not at all incompatible with their own—although his humor may have been a little disconcerting to them, since, despite its inherent absurdity, life is, after all, not supposed to be *funny*.

Roger Shattuck's book *The Banquet Years* came along in 1955 and introduced Jarry as a persona to the general reading public. Prior to this, the non-French-speaking reader had virtually no access to Jarry, despite the fact that there was a wealth of Jarry material available in French, including several biographies and various incomplete "Oeuvres Completes." However, with the arrival of *The Selected Works of Alfred Jarry* in 1965, it finally became possible for those whose appetites had been whetted by *The Banquet Years* and the *Evergreen Review* articles to see for themselves just who the man behind Jarry's absurd and *outré* disguise really was.

The Selected Works and *The Banquet Years* provided a whole new generation of future artists and writers with exposure to Jarry. Coming of age during the 1960s, bludgeoned by the pointless carnage of the Vietnam war on the six o'clock news, and faced with increasing meaninglessness in daily life as a result of a rapidly-disintegrating society, this group has found Jarry to be a 19th-century forerunner of the present age: the patron saint of modern irrationality. His sensibilities are clearly visible in a great deal of the writing, music, and art being produced today, whether by direct influence or intellectual osmosis. This book, for instance, is the work of two people on whom Jarry has been a primary influence: myself and illustrator Bill Griffith. In the Introduction I have already described my own relationship to Jarry and his work. As for Griffith, he was an art student during the sixties, innocently planning a future career as an abstract expressionist, when he happened to encounter Jarry in the pages of *The Banquet Years*. Not long thereafter he took off impulsively for Paris without a return ticket; back in New York he subsequently became an underground cartoonist and (not surprisingly) began to focus on the baffling and amusing irrationality that characterizes modern life. He has used Jarry as a recurring character in a number of strips, and has done missionary work for Jarry's questionable cause in the form of a pictoral Jarry biography in *Raw* magazine. A pataphysical flavor permeates much of Griffith's work, especially the antics of Zippy the Pinhead, his best-known character. (There are even those who suggest that the bulky, pointy-headed, loosely-gowned Zippy resembles a benevolent Ubu, and that the entropical pinhead's unique brand of disconnected "reality" has more than a touch of the pataphysical in it.)

Today Jarry's absurdist spirit can be sensed in many places. Not surprisingly, *Ubu* productions are numerous; one such production ran in Los Angeles for more than six months in 1982, playing to capacity crowds. Other "Ubus" crop up with regularity, sometimes in highly unlikely locations: Bill Griffith recently saw an announcement for a limited run of *Ubu* in a neighborhood Catholic church in San Francisco! Tributes to Jarry come in many forms; for instance, there is an FM station in Santa Cruz, California, which calls itself KUSP—"Pataphysical Radio"; and a punk band, comprised of art students from the Midwest, has dubbed itself "Père Ubu."

Jarry has left an indelible stamp on the art of the 20th century, from Cubism to the Theater of the Absurd. Yet despite Apollinaire's obvious respect for the pataphysician from Laval, I beg to disagree with him: Jarry was not "the last sublime debauchee of the Renaissance." Considering the political, social, and artistic developments of the past twenty-five years, Jarry is only beginning to come into his own: he is the first sublime humorist of the Apocalypse.

The Pataphysician:
An Imaginary Solution

Fiction by Nigey Lennon

One Friday evening, Mary Ann Utterly toiled up the worn and sagging stairs to her Hollywood apartment with sore feet and an aching soul. It is only fair to point out that Mary Ann was ordinarily a steadfastly cheerful girl, a complete stranger to fits of existential despair; but at this particular moment life had never seemed so bleak and insupportable, nor the breaks so inequitably distributed. From start to finish, her day had been a calamity—or rather a series of calamities, beginning innocently enough with snagged pantyhose, continuing through bounced checks and editorial snafus, escalating to include a canceled date with an old flame who was not due back in town for at least another six months, and culminating in an annoying (and costly) vehicular breakdown on the Santa Ana Freeway right in the middle of the so-called "rush" hour. Now, with the day's tribulations seemingly over, the only surefire antidote to such gut-level misery appeared to be alcoholic, and although Mary Ann tended towards moderation in her vices, under the circumstances she was more than ready to throw moderation to the four winds.

"Well, at least I'm home," she said to herself as she put her key in the door. As if on cue, the key stuck in the lock, and when she tried to force it, she suddenly found herself holding the rounded end of the key in her hand while meanwhile regarding its long flimsy shaft still protruding from the keyhole. It had snapped clean off.

After a frustrating interval of useless fumbling, during which it became manifestly apparent that Mary Ann had absolutely no future as a locksmith, she was obliged to admit that her next stop must be the apartment of her landlady, Mrs. Scruggs. Mary Ann had been avoiding such an encounter due to a certain delicacy born of bouncing checks and editorial snafus, but somehow the romantic notion of spending an *al fresco* evening under the stars held no appeal for her on this particular humid, smoggy night. Reluctantly, but with an outward invincibility born of desperation, she marched herself down to Mrs. Scruggs's apartment, rang the doorbell and, when that lady made her appearance, demanded the passkey.

"You're three weeks late with your rent," observed Mrs. Scruggs, also as if on cue. Mary Ann mumbled an assent, appended an unintelligible alibi, seized the passkey from her landlady's bony claw, and fled before any further discussion could arise.

Luckily there were no more difficulties concerning lock or key, and at long last Mary Ann staggered through the front door and into her bedroom, where she began peeling off her clothes with a gratitude that approached worship. Hungering for the warm comfort of her motley old bathrobe, she hastened to the closet. The mail could wait; it had a monotonous tendency to repeat critical comments from collection agencies anyway. The light on the answering machine was flashing, indicating that there were messages awaiting her attention, but in the masochistic luxury of her bone weariness, she chose to ignore them too.

She had yanked the homey flannel garment out of her closet and was standing there nude, on one foot, about to wriggle into it, when seemingly out of nowhere a strange and distinctly rusty-sounding male voice suddenly droned: "Ma-dame, please have the de-cen-cy to dis-robe be-hind the clo-set door. The sight of so much fe-male pul-chri-tude fills us with loath-ing."

Stricken by sheer befuddlement, Mary Ann let her bathrobe fall to the floor and whirled sharply around to ascertain the source of this most unexpected comment. The sight that met her popping eyes plunged her even more deeply into confusion. For there, in the furthermost corner of the bedroom, stood an uncommonly short, swarthy, stockily-built man, in age perhaps somewhere between twenty-five and thirty years old. His hair was a dense thatch of stick-straight ebony, parted squarely in the middle; beneath beetling dark brows his luminous jet-black eyes, sunk deeply in an alarmingly pale face, snapped and glinted with the sudden malevolence of summer lighting. His garb was outlandish: torn canvas shoes, baggy nondescript trousers rolled up and stuffed into grimy gray stockings, and a ragged cyclist's racing jersey with the grandiose inscription "Grand Prix de Chandelle Vert 1896" emblazoned rather incongruously across its grease-spattered chest. The apparition's right hand was resting on the worn leather saddle of an ancient bicycle, which sported a punctured and sagging rear tire. But of more immediate concern to Mary Ann was his left hand, which was tightly clasped around the handle of a small, long-muzzled dueling pistol. This weapon (whose mate, unbeknownst to Mary Ann, reposed in the intruder's back trouser pocket) was pointing directly at her.

"Well, good grief!" she spluttered, but the apparition raised his right hand from the bicycle seat—an extremely mechanical gesture—and cut her off in mid-splutter with a truculent remark. "So much ad-i-pose tis-sue is not at all to our li-king. We warn you, Ma-dame, we are an ex-cel-lent shot, and you can see for your-self that it is no great dis-tance be-tween your ri-dic-u-lous per-son and our-self, ev-en if this piece of i-di-ot fur-ni-ture is in the di-rect path of our tra-jec-to-ry." This was delivered in a monontonous, evenly-stressed tone which nonetheless managed to sound extremely disparaging despite its lack of expression. The piece of "i-di-ot fur-ni-ture" in question happened to be a white vanity table with chintz skirts that Mary Ann had received in bygone years as a junior high school graduation present—a trifle insipid perhaps, and certainly jejeune, but not precisely idiotic. It was this bizarre and nasty dig at Mary Ann's treasured girlhood which caused her ire to rise until it completely sub-merged her fear. Stooping quickly, she slid into her bathrobe and then, straightening up, proceeded to march briskly across the few feet of space between her and the intruder. Towering over him like a conquering Val-kyrie, she shook a delicately tapered forefinger under his nose and de-manded, ''Who are you? And just what, may I ask, are you doing here?'' (It crossed her mind that this might be a henchman of Mrs. Scruggs's, although he seemed to have some weird kind of accent and Mrs. Scruggs had never rented to a foreigner yet.)

''We might ve-ry well ask you the same ques-tion, Ma-dame,'' retorted the apparition, but he relaxed his grip on the pistol slightly, although he didn't retreat.

''This is my apartment,'' snapped Mary Ann. ''At least, I mean it is unless Mrs. Scruggs sent you to change the lock or something. What are you—a burglar?''

''Ma-dame,'' sniffed the intruder with every indication of outraged dig-nity, ''you can see ve-ry well for your-self that there is no-thing here worth the bo-ther of steal-ing. But since it is be-com-ing in-creas-ing-ly clear to us that you are in-ca-pa-ble of un-der-stan-ding e-ven the sim-plest of ex-pla-na-tions, we will there-fore of-fer you a more com-plex one.'' He smiled darkly, set the pistol down on the top of a nearby nightstand, which matched the ''idiot'' vanity table, and pointed a commanding finger toward his bicycle with its flat tire. ''Our ma-chine—as e-ven you can see—sus-tained an in-ju-ry, and we were thus forced by this most ab-surd cir-cum-stance to stop some-where to re-pair it.''

Mary Ann stared hard at him. Nothing he was saying made any sense at all, but he really didn't seem to be a burglar, even if he did have a gun. It was far more likely that he had come from the county mental health clinic a few blocks away. The facility's outpatients could often be seen shuffling along the streets of the neighborhood, looking straight ahead and mumbling to themselves about how Liberace was sending them secret messages through the overhead telephone wires. The method by which the bizarre little intruder had gotten into her apartment seemed rather mysterious, but his dirty old clothes and his idiosyncratic manner of speaking seemed to place him squarely in the camp of the mentally un-balanced rather than the ranks of the criminally-inclined. The main thing, she realized, was to get him out of the apartment before some trifling detail or other offended him and he wound up expressing his dis-satisfaction with that damn pistol of his. Hopefully the eviction could be accomplished in a firm but friendly manner, without calling the police; after all, Mary Ann had been a psych major in junior college.

"Look, I'm sorry your bicycle broke down," she began in what she hoped was a conciliatory, but not patronizing, tone, "but you really can't fix it here; that would make too big a mess, and I don't have a bicycle pump anyway. But there's a gas station on the corner that you could take it to—"

"Our ma-chine is com-plete-ly pat-a-phys-i-cal," intoned the apparition solemnly. "Since it o-per-ates on pat-a-phys-i-cal prin-ci-ples, the in-take or ex-change of an-y gas-es would be en-ti-re-ly su-per-flu-ous. No, Ma-dame, what we re-qui-re is not gas, but ra-ther a man-ner of re-stor-ing the for-mer ro-tun-di-ty to that which rolls." Jerkily, he thrust out an arm toward the bicycle's flat tire.

"Oh Lord," sighed Mary Ann. This was going to be far more difficult than she had envisioned. And something else had crossed her mind, too: "Who's this 'we' you keep talking about?" she demanded. "Do you have some partner who's hiding in the bushes outside, waiting for you to give him a signal?"

"Al-low us to in-tro-duce our-self," announced the peculiar little fellow, drawing himself up to his full four-foot-nine with the mechanical bombast of an automaton. "We are Mon-sieur Al-fred Jar-ry, man of let-ters from Par-is, cel-e-brated pat-a-phys-i-cian and phi-lo-so-pher." Upon completing this speech, he marched over to Mary Ann's bed and collapsed on it, falling stiffly with his limbs splayed out in four different directions, and remaining exactly where he fell. In that position he resembled a tin soldier with arthritis. "We will have some ab-sinthe now," he added imperatively, glaring up at Mary Ann from the bed.

"Absonth?" she repeated. She dimly remembered having once read about some evil brew that went by that name—it had been considered so nasty and dangerous that it had finally been outlawed, even in France. But even if she'd just happened to have had some lying around, she certainly wouldn't have offered it to this outrageous maniac. Who knows to what new depths of depravity he would have sunk under its vile and pernicious influence?

"Look," she said, "I don't have any absonth, but I'm going to make a phone call, and you and your goddamn bicycle had both be out of here before I'm finished, or—or—" She couldn't think of anything sufficiently ominous-sounding to finish up with, so she stamped out of the bedroom in what she desperately hoped was an intimidating fashion.

"As you wish, Ma-dame," Monsieur Alfred Jarry growled deprecat-ingly, waving his hand in the air and closing his eyes. But he didn't budge an inch.

In the living room, Mary Ann slumped over on the couch and dialed Tom Wetherly's phone number. Tom was a good friend of hers, a reporter on the Los Angeles *Tribune*. His news beat for that paper encompassed lunatics of all sorts. Whenever a new guru suddenly blew into Glendale, for instance, prophesying the end of the world at precisely 3:24 p.m. on Wednesday the nineteenth, Tom would be summarily dispatched to find out the fakir's particulars, including favorite color and whether or not the holy person liked Olivia Newton-John. If upon cordial interrogation the aforementioned seer lapsed into sullen silence and refused to reveal his exalted secrets to the uncouth and unspiritual Western dog of journalism, Wetherly would note the nature of the guru's temporal surroundings and the precise shade of his robe, and would then proceed to flesh out the rest of his story with witty asides, although without shirking for a moment the crucial subject of the guru's finances. This was a formula which had made him virtually indispensable to the otherwise predictable and pedestrian *Tribune*. Wetherly was well aware of his value, and as a result his work hours were correspondingly irregular.

Luckily for Mary Ann, he happened to be at home on this particular Friday night, nursing a hangover and running a favorite episode of ''Masterpiece Theatre'' on his video recorder. He had taken the day off work and, being a sociable fellow, was growing very bored with only himself for company. Despite the fact that his was essentially a cerebral nature and Mary Ann seemed to prefer volleyball to intellectual activity, he was not insensitive to her considerable charms, and when she told him that there was a certifiable nut holed up in her apartment, his professional ears pricked up as well. ''I'll grab a bottle of wine and be right over,'' he promised.

When he arrived at Mary Ann's apartment a mere thirty minutes later, he was greeted by a most unusual tableau. In the kitchen area, a small but fierce-looking figure was perching precariously on a wicker bar stool, glowering and grinding out a static series of seemingly incomprehensible monosyllables like a Cuisinart running amok. A cursory glance revealed that his feet didn't even touch the floor. The moment Tom walked through the door, Mary Ann dragged him into a corner and hissed, ''You've got to help me get rid of him! He's got a gun!''

Wetherly was instantly intrigued. ''Leave it to me,'' he assured Mary Ann. Then, walking over to where the miniature menace was roosting, he held out his hand in a genial manner. ''My name's Tom Wetherly,'' he boomed. Alfred Jarry paused in the midst of his mechanical monologue and fastened his snapping black eyes on Wetherly's lanky form towering high above him. ''What is that to us, mon-sieur?'' he growled. ''We did not ask you for an in-tro-duc-tion. We were en-gaged in at-temp-ting to ob-tain some-thing to drink from this most un-gra-cious fe-male here.''

Wetherly immediately presented the bottle of chablis that was tucked under his arm. "I think I can solve that problem, at least," he observed. "Here you go, uh—"

"Our name is Al-fred Jar-ry," said the little automaton, bowing stiffly from the waist. "And we thank you, mon-sieur, for hav-ing more com-mon sense than this ri-dic-u-lous fe-male. She sim-ply does not ap-pear to un-der-stand that we have had an ex-treme-ly stren-u-ous jour-ney, and that we are in great need of li-quid sus-te-nance." He seized the wine from Tom and demanded, "Is there such a thing as a screw in this mis-er-a-ble me-nage?"

Tom held back a chuckle as Mary Ann glared. "You're filthy-minded as well as crazy," she observed acidly, but Wetherly deposited himself on the stool next to Jarry's and proceeded to break off the plastic seal that enclosed the bottle cap. "You don't need a corkscrew for these babies," he explained as he twisted the cap off. "Miracles of modern science and all that." Jarry watched him with glinting eyes. "We are a sci-en-tist our-self," he said, "and we beg to in-form you that there are no mi-ra-cles in sci-ence, only hy-po-the-ses, the-o-ries and laws. Mi-ra-cles are the swill of ro-man-tic tip-plers to whom the ab-so-lute lo-gic of ab-sinthe is an ab-om-i-na-tion." This speech had apparently made him thirstier than ever, for he grabbed the jug of wine, ignoring the glasses that Mary Ann had grudgingly set down on the bar in front of him. While Tom and Mary Ann stared at him incredulously, he open-throated half of the bottle's contents without pausing for breath, then set down the bottle and wiped his lips on his grubby sleeve. "It is quite young and pre-sump-tu-ous," he observed, gesturing at the bottle, "and it has a dis-tinct af-ter-taste of cre-o-sote. Quite clear-ly it comes from the sea-ward slopes of Tur-ki-stan, where the fel-luc-cas sweep a-cross the Bos-phor-ous and the fol-lo-wers of No-stra-da-mus se-cret-ly stu-dy the Ca-bal-a in the cool pil-lared la-by-rinths of the Cas-bah." He trailed off into a series of grunts, like a machine gradually running out of steam, then reapplied himself with vigor to the young and presumptuous, but apparently tolerable, wine.

Tom and Mary Ann exchanged a pregnant glance. "It sounds like you have an accent," began Tom good-naturedly. "Where are you from, Al?"

"We are from Par-is," Jarry replied curtly, swallowing in haste. "And we do not wish to be re-ferred to as 'Al,' mon-sieur. It is not pat-a-phys-i-cal to shor-ten the tan-gent-ial planes of ob-jects—on-ly to lengthen-en them."

Tom leaned back and attempted to digest the *outré* performance of this seedy but imperious midget, from his royal "we" to his pseudo-scientific ramblings. Jarry's manner of speech was easily the weirdest Wetherly had ever encountered in fifteen solid years of interviewing weirdos—it resembled an ancient and cranky merry-go-round in desperate need of grease more than it did the mellifluous inflections of French. From whence, Tom wondered, sprung the shrimp's colossal arrogance? And more importantly, from which mental institution had he escaped? With reportorial zeal, he decided to probe deeper into this fascinating anomaly.

Several bottles of wine and a number of hours later, Wetherly was a great deal wiser about the ostensible M. Jarry. Sitting at his desk in the *Tribune* city room the next morning, he attempted to decipher his hastily-scribbled notes from the previous night: "Born Brittany 1873, whiz kid high school, arrived Paris age 17, dressed in bizarre costumes & affected eccentric behavior, hung out w/Rousseau, Picasso, etc., invented pseudo-science called ' 'Pataphysique' . . ." The notes became increasingly indecipherable toward the end. Wetherly shook his aching head as he recalled some of the previous night's events: how Jarry, seemingly sober as a judge after three bottles of wine, had observed that "this bev-er-age could use some im-prove-ment," and had marched over to Mary Ann's refrigerator, where he had found (shudder!) a jar of mayonnaise reposing on the shelf. A generous dollop of this oleaginous substance had been deposited in his glass of wine; the liquid and the solid were mixed together with a scientific, if grimy, forefinger; and the resultingly murky combination was drunk down with an impassive countenance and an approving smack of the lips. "It will do," the manic mixologist had remarked. "It all de-pends on the de-gree of one's thirst: we have no-ted that, in the ab-sence of drink, thirst is in-creased by a pow-er of four. Once in Par-is we took a glass of ab-sinthe, vin-e-gar and In-di-a ink, and our thirst was mul-ti-plied a hun-dred-fold."

Tom chuckled softly to himself. Obviously this fellow, whoever he was, was crazy as the proverbial loon. And yet Wetherly was troubled by something vague and distant, some dim notion that disturbed the surface of his thoughts like a tiny pebble thrown into a vast reservoir. He had studied French Lit in college, some twenty-five years ago, and like all required subjects it had oozed into and then out of his consciousness, leaving hardly any residue behind; but still, the things Mary Ann's bizarre little intruder had told him had their own strange cohesiveness. If this was the monologue of a deranged mind, it also had some elements of genius in it. What ordinary madman had such command of language, such an ability to string together ideas, however disconnected they ultimately were? Not that there was any way, of course, that the guy could really be a hundred and ten years old—he appeared to be in his early thirties—and his story about having avoided death through the application of "pataphysical principles" only reinforced Wetherly's initial impression that the lights were on, but nobody was home. And yet, at the end of the evening (just before a rather inebriated Wetherly had, no doubt foolishly, agreed to allow Jarry to spend the night at his apartment), the miniature maniac had solemnly pulled a wad of franc notes out of his pocket, insisting that Wetherly accept them as payment for the wine. On close inspection, the notes appeared to be genuine, bearing dates of 1898 and 1902. Yes, reflected Wetherly, if this was a shtick, it was an incredibly well-planned one, and definitely worth a short feature in the *Tribune*. He put his notes aside, switched on the terminal of his word processor, and keyed in his slugline: "Alfred Jarry in L.A."

Perhaps inevitably, Tom Wetherly and Alfred Jarry soon became roommates. Wetherly was never sure exactly how Jarry stage-managed such a rapid rise from the lowly status of one-shot overnight guest to the exalted position of absolute monarch of the apartment, but it happened almost before he knew it. In no time at all, Jarry had become a permanent fixture around the place, and the bachelor pad's sole closet had become a repository for Jarry's bicycle, fishing gear, odds and ends of clothing, and indescribable flotsam and jetsam.

As an easygoing bachelor with little interest in suburban-style virtues, Wetherly had never been particularly conscientious about his domestic engineering, but after a few days of living in a single room with a dedicated nihilist like Jarry, Tom began to regard his former habits as virtually Good-Housekeeping-approved by comparison. Jarry was capable of such charming gestures as leaving dead fish lying around for days at a stretch— or worse, of depositing them among the shoes in the cramped and tiny closet, there to ripen and bloom into exquisite fragrance. When Tom testily confronted his pint-sized lodger with the smelly evidence, Jarry cocked an eyebrow and commented, "You must not con-demn the time-hon-ored prac-ti-ces of o-ther cul-tures. In Ma-da-gas-car all fish are placed in co-vered con-tain-ers and left in the sum-mer sun un-til the flesh falls from the bones. Then they are ea-ten raw and whole with great gus-to, for it is on-ly then that the na-tives con-si-der them pre-pared *à point*." It was impossible to refute such inverse logic; Tom soon learned not even to bother trying. He decided that living with the stench was a far easier task than attempting to dispute Jarry's pataphysical premises.

There were other discrepancies as well. If Wetherly's hours were erratic, then Jarry's were positively perverse. He enjoyed sitting up all night scribbling madly (in what appeared to be genuine French, Wetherly noted), fueled by copious draughts of liquor, while meanwhile the lights blazed until morning. To make Tom's nightmares even worse, when Jarry wrote he invariably had a transistor radio tuned to an AM talk station; meanwhile the FM receiver was pulling in a Mexican polka program, and the TV spewed forth all-night horror movies or, for a change of pace, the oratory of a pompadoured evangelist on cable. Jarry was a born vidiot; television (which he professed never to have seen before) completely mesmerized him. The moment he came striding into the apartment, he would promptly switch on the tube. His favorite viewing schedule tended to consist of random channel roulette with the cable selector box, ping-ponging from one channel to another at ten-second intervals. "If we ev-er re-turn to Par-is we shall sure-ly take one of these with us," he told Tom, indicating the selector box. "It is the ul-ti-mate pat-a-phys-i-cal de-vice. Where else can one view a do-mes-tic al-ter-ca-tion, a Be-dou-in tramp-ing a-cross the Si-nai, an a-do-les-cent fe-male in the throes of est-rus, a ga-lax-y in e-rup-tion and an ad-ver-tise-ment for de-o-dor-ant all in the blink of an eye?"

Wetherly was not at all sure why he continued to tolerate the minuscule madman's presence under his roof, but whenever he felt a strong temptation to throw Jarry out, he also found himself feeling strangely guilty. For beneath the mad midget's brusque and bizarre exterior, there was also a capacity for sudden affectionate gestures which seemed to surprise him as much as they surprised Tom. Try though he would to disguise it, Jarry appeared to be growing genuinely fond of his benefactor. From time to time Tom would discover oddball items lying on top of the chest of drawers, and knew that they had been left there for him to find: some verses in French, which Wetherly couldn't read; half a bottle of wine (ordinarily Jarry never left any liquor bottle unturned); the flattened pelt of an unfortunate bird Jarry had thought was especially interesting, and which he had painstakingly picked over and cleaned until the rough underside was smooth and the feathers gleaming. When Tom tried to thank his benefactor for his gifts, Jarry merely snorted. "Eh! It is no-thing, mere-ly some tri-fle we had no use for," he would snap, looking away in feigned disgust. But in a day or two another such offering would be laid on the chest, and sooner or later another.

Jarry had no visible means of support, and the only funds he seemed to possess were the antique franc notes in his pocket, which understandably didn't go very far. Yet he insisted on being as independent as he could under the circumstances. Most of the time he flatly refused to share

Tom's food, seeming to prefer the fish he caught on his frequent jaunts to the L.A. River (he was able to catch fish anywhere), or the small birds he shot in the neighborhood's trees. One evening Tom came home from work to find Jarry bustling fiercely about the apartment's tiny kitchen, a ludicrous sight in an improvised bedsheet apron which dragged on the floor, constantly tripping him up. He had scrawled across the apron in his favorite India ink, "Chef de Merdre." As Tom watched, half amused and half horrified, Jarry opened the oven door with a flourish and extracted a meat loaf pan in which reposed the burnt carcasses of three small birds. "Two Eng-lish spar-rows and a mock-ing-bird," he recited grandly, "de-feath-ered, dis-em-bow-eled and dis-em-brained, and roas-ted af-ter the fash-ion of the First Mar-grave of Lich-ten-stein." Extending the pan to Tom with a mechanical bow, he added, *"Bon ap-pe-tit."*

Jarry had been Tom's roommate for a couple of weeks (Tom was still trying to figure out how to get rid of him, and was finding the solution to be well nigh pataphysical) when Weatherly's feature article about him showed up in the *Tribune*. When Mary Ann Utterly picked up the Trib to read it with her morning coffee, she found the story smack dab in the middle of the front page of the metro news section. It was adorned with a two-column-wide photo of Jarry in a video game arcade, scowling into the camera as he stood before the hypnotic display of a Donkey Kong machine. Tom Wetherly had employed a clever tactic; he had written the story from Jarry's point of view, letting the sheer outrageousness of the belligerent shrimp's patter speak for itself. Jarry was quoted as saying that he intended to make a good long stay in Los Angeles, as "it is beau-ty it-self. It is an-cient Rome, but with-out a heart. It is mod-ern. It is com-plete-ly and thor-ough-ly ir-ra-tion-al. It cap-ti-vates and nau-se-ates us. We will per-haps pitch a tent in the ex-act cen-ter of San-ta Mon-i-ca Bou-le-vard . . .''

Wetherly had also described without editorial comment the visitor's fascination with video games and his praise for Los Angeles's "na-tive cui-sine," especially delicacies like Cool Whip, bubble gum modeled in the shape of tacos and the surreal extrusions of fast-food franchises. Then he went on to describe how Jarry had, through the science of pataphysics, claimed to have bypassed his own death. "We left Par-is on No-vem-ber first, nine-teen-aught-sev-en," Jarry explained, "and passed in-to e-ther-ni-ty. We have been trav-el-ing ev-er since."

"We had al-ways put off com-ing to A-mer-i-ca," the story quoted Jarry in conclusion, "but now that we have ar-rived in its ve-ry heart, as it were, we will ad-mit that we are in-clined to re-main. It is true that we can-not ob-tain a con-ge-ni-al glass of ab-sinthe an-y-where in the ci-ty; and there are no li-ter-a-ry jour-nals in which to pro-pound our most im-por-tant the-o-ries; but the free-ways sup-ply a most re-gal sur-face for the pas-sage of our ex-al-ted bi-cy-cle, and we find the con-stant pre-sence of that en-chan-ting sub-stance com-mon-ly re-fer-red to as 'smog' odd-ly in-vi-go-ra-ting.''

Five minutes after Mary Ann had dazedly finished perusing this piece of journalism, the phone rang. It was Tom Wetherly. Gone was his usual hearty bluffness and self-possession; now his voice was weak with desper-ation. ''Mary Ann,'' he wheezed, ''you've got to help me. Ever since the damn article hit the street, my phone's been ringing off the hook with people who insist on talking to Alfred. Apparently some idiot operator on the Trib switchboard got fed up with taking messages for me, and since it was my day off she started giving out my home number! And that's not the worst by a long shot! There are a million goddamn rubbernecks swarming around my apartment building, trying to catch a glimpse of Al—dunno how they found out where I lived, but here they are. One goon just stuck his head right through the front window, hoping to see something, although I can't for the life of me imagine what—and Al calmly took a shot at him with his pistol! Luckily the fool yanked his head out again before the bullet got to him, or I'd have a lawsuit on my hands.''

''How's Alfred taking all the excitement otherwise?'' asked Mary Ann weakly.

''That's just the problem! He absolutely adores the attention! When the first clump of people showed up and started milling around a while ago, he walked out onto the balcony announcing, 'We must not ne-glect our sub-jects.' And of course the sight of him just drove the crowd bananas! Now he's standing out there like the Pope giving an audience, inciting them to riot for all I know, and the rubbernecks keep going to the pay phone at the liquor store up the street and telling all their frigging friends to hurry over and see the circus! If it keeps up I dunno what's going to hap-pen! Can you get over here right away? You introduced me to him, for Christ's sake!''

In no time at all, the media career of Alfred Jarry, self-professed man of letters from Paris, had taken off like a pataphysical skyrocket. After the appearance of the *Tribune* article, the bemused Wetherly began to be deluged, both at home and at work, by calls from people requesting inter-views or other audiences with Jarry. Local TV and radio stations, publi-cations ranging from the extremely esoteric to the steadfastly ordinary, fast-buck promoters, wide-eyed nymphets who wanted to start Alfred Jarry fan clubs—they were all suddenly beating a path to Wetherly's door. He had no idea why Jarry seemed to strike such a responsive chord in the general public, but since Alfred himself was far from averse to publicity, Tom accordingly adopted the role of agent and started booking him on

TV and radio programs. If John Travolta could be sold to the general public, then anything was possible, he reflected cynically. At least Alfred was an astute if somewhat eccentric rhetoritician.

When the limelight was aimed in his direction, Jarry never failed to put on a show. He cut a strange and ludicrous figure on the six o'clock news in a rusty black suit two sizes too big for him, with his ferocious scowl and the rushing torrent of his disconnected thoughts. Although his irrational and sullen behavior horrified some of the older, more conventional members of the media, he was an instant hit with younger people. One of the arty weekly newspapers around town immediately proclaimed Jarry its official mascot, with huge headlines on the front page heralding him as "The Spirit of Modern Times." Its arch rival felt compelled to respond by running a column in each issue that detailed Jarry's comings, goings, and various eccentric gestures—much of it fictional, of course.

Jarry took all this glory as his divine right, delighting in fueling the fire with ever more flamboyant public behavior. While bicycling around the west side of town one night, he grew thirsty and stopped at a notorious swingers' watering hole in Marina del Rey. His fame, of course, had preceeded him there, and when he strode through the door of the saloon, its tanned and muscular clientele began flocking around him, eager to demonstrate their hipness by paying him court. Some of them offered to buy him drinks, while others tried to lure him into the bathrooms with seductive promises of cocaine, but although he accepted their attention with his customarily brusque *noblesse oblige*, he refused all drinks, toots, and other inducements, and strode jerkily up to the bar, where he demanded a liter of absinthe.

"Absonth," those in the know chuckled together. "Ha-ha—what a character!" (The saloon, although it prided itself on being somewhat *nouvelle*, naturally did not stock absinthe—although as Jarry's notoriety increased, unscrupulous barkeeps all over town began shamelessly pawning off execrable counterfeit concoctions of their own as that most celebrated distillation.)

The trouble began when a female Arnold Schwarzenegger came steamrolling toward the bar, where Jarry was obliviously immersing himself in a curious mixture of his own—Vandermint liqueur and tomato juice. "Bartender, give the man a Harvey Wallbanger," she ordered, waving an arm whose biceps resembled a buffalo hump. As the bartender hesitated, looking questioningly from Jarry to the would-be benefactress, Jarry put down his glass and scowled up at her with icy eyes. "Ma-dame," he sneered, "e-ven if you were a la-dy we would not ac-cept the wa-ter of life from you. We do not like wo-men at all, es-pec-i-al-ly when they dis-turb our no-ble train of thought with tri-vi-al in-ter-rup-tions.''

"Oh yeah? Whaddaya say you and me step outside and settle the score, Jack?'' she sneered back at him, suddenly transformed from a genial sycophant into a raging six-foot hellion.

Without warning, Jarry slipped his hand into the pocket of his baggy pants and yanked out his ubiquitous pistol. There was a profound and resonant gasp from the watching crowd as he coolly raised the weapon and aimed it at the exact spot in the mirror behind the bar where the of-fending woman was reflected. "Va-ni-ty is the fee-ble shield of the im-po-tent a-gainst the me-di-oc-ri-ty of death,'' he growled, and pulling the trigger, proceeded to blast the glass of the mirror into a spinning spider-web of imploding crystal shards. Chaos and anarchy immediately took over, and by the time the hubbub finally subsided, Jarry had vanished into the night. (The muscular female was found lying on the floor beside the bar, having fainted dead away.)

As the Jarry fad threatened to reach epidemic proportions, trendy shops on Melrose Avenue began doing a roaring trade in sweatshirts decorated with his scowling image. These rapidly became absolutely *de rigueur* for anyone with any pretensions to artistic sophistication. Then an enterpris-ing art student created half a dozen suitably nihilistic Jarry postcards. Shortly thereafter, Tom Wetherly started getting calls from the owners of punk night clubs, asking if Jarry would be willing to make personal ap-pearances. A punk band even recorded a tribute to Jarry, aptly entitled "We Hate L.A.''; it was instantly added to the playlist of the local com-mercial punk station, and began rapidly selling out in record stores all over town. It seemed only a matter of time before some hotshot promoter would step up and ask Wetherly for the franchise rights to the Jarry im-age, and the inevitable Alfred Jarry coffee mugs and key chains would start flooding the gift shops and drugstores.

Probably the entire Jarry media blitz, like any other overnight sensa-tion, would have evaporated sooner or later, were it not for a sudden strange turn of events. Jarry's unlooked-for arrival in Los Angeles had oc-curred near the climax of a very tense municipal election. Mayor James C. Goodfellow, the incumbent, had served two terms, but the prospects for his re-election were looking very bleak indeed. Goodfellow, a Demo-crat, suffered the misfortune of being an urbane and moderate gentleman in a primitive and senseless age. He no longer had an actively supportive constituency, because he was considered too wishy-washy by many of the left-leaning Democrats, and dangerously radical by those tending toward the middle of the spectrum. No one seemed to like him anymore, even though his record during the past two terms had been virtually spotless.

When he campaigned in Hollywood, young punks with blue hair yelled at him, "Go home, Grandpa, and drink your damn martinis! This is a whole new world!" And when he spoke before Rotary meetings, vacuum cleaner salesmen in seersucker suits worried that Goodfellow and his fellow city council members were sending daily radio reports to Moscow and duly receiving instructions to institute tougher rent control measures. Sometimes Goodfellow wondered if he had a friend left in the world.

As election day drew ominously nearer, Goodfellow and his campaign aides became correspondingly more despondent. Voter turnout was likely to be at an all-time low, and the advance polls showed that Goodfellow's chief opponent, Marshall Law, was running ahead by a two-to-one margin. When it came to young hooligans with blue hair, the hard-line Republican Law didn't cut them any slack. The only blue hair he understood was on the heads of his elderly female supporters—the ones who kept sawed-off shotguns in their cedar chests, knowing full well that it was only a matter of time before the ghetto youths arrived to rape and pillage. Law's campaign platform consisted of three very simple planks: More money for big business. Less money for frivolity (i.e., public transit, city parks, libraries, weekly garbage pickup, etc.). And, of course, law and order. "My name isn't Law for nothing," he bellowed as his supporters cheered. "When I'm elected, I'll make this a law-abiding city again, no foolin'!" There was, unfortunately, no reason to doubt him.

Election day was only three weeks away when one morning Goodfellow's campaign manager Dana Dewitt happened to switch on his TV while getting dressed for work. There on the "AM LA" show was none other than Alfred Jarry, scowling away as usual and exuding his disconnected philosophy of life in macerated monosyllables. A film clip showed the baggy-suited shrimp pedaling down Sunset Boulevard on his bicycle, narrowly missing a disastrous collision with a Hostess bakery truck. Then he was shown surrounded by numerous admiring hipsters at a Melrose Avenue punk club. "With his bizarre and mechanical behavior, Alfred Jarry stands as a biting one-man commentary on the sheer confusion and irrationality of modern life," explained the show's hostess. "He claims to have been a well-known writer in turn-of-the-century Paris, and that he bypassed his death seventy-four years ago after discovering the science of ' 'Pataphysics.' Of course his admirers find this sort of thing very amusing because it's all part of the absurdity of the Jarry myth—or in-joke."

Dewitt paused in the act of shaving and peered a little more closely at the TV screen. He was intrigued by the absoluteness of Jarry's declamations. They didn't make any sense, but they were delivered with the incontestable resonance and solemnity of pronouncements from on high. Undoubtedly the man was a mental case, but most of the politicians Dewitt had run across tended to fall into that category in one way or another. He grinned ruefully as he remarked to himself, "I'd take an Alfred Jarry over a Ronald Reagan any day—hands down. At least Jarry can *act*."

Thoughts of Jarry continued to percolate in his mind as he drove to City Hall. He had a meeting with Goodfellow at ten o'clock, and by the time he walked briskly into the mayor's office, a plan was already beginning to form itself in the nether depths of his subconscious. "James," he began, glancing over at the haggard features of his hopeless chief, "I think there may be a way we can turn this goddamn campaign around." Then he began to outline a bold and downright shocking plan to Goodfellow, Dewitt's enthusiasm growing as the details fell into place.

Within an hour Dewitt was on the phone to Tom Wetherly, whom he had known since Wetherly had been on the *Tribune*'s city hall beat some years previously. Within another hour, Jarry was in Mayor Goodfellow's office. The mayor crouched warily behind his desk, outwardly cordial but inwardly dubious. Dwarfed by the massiveness of a very dignified and judicial leather armchair, Jarry sat twitching erratically like a faultily-wired robot. Dewitt did all the talking as a thoroughly tickled Wetherly strained himself to keep from laughing. Jarry's media career had been extremely amusing to date, but if Wetherly understood Dana Dewitt's proposition, then this was its crowning moment of absurdist glory: Jarry had been offered the deputy mayorship of Los Angeles.

But as soon as Jarry grasped the nature of Dewitt's offer, his sullen intractability became verbal. "We do not wish to en-gage in such pet-ti-ness," he grumbled, shaking his head. "Such mat-ters are best left in the hands of those with no cour-age. This ci-ty hall of yours is a re-mar-ka-bly ug-ly buil-ding an-y-way, and we have no wish to be forced to in-ha-bit it."

"But think of all the attention you'd get," argued Dewitt, pandering to what he assumed were Jarry's basest instincts. "Imagine all the publicity that'll be directed at you once Mayor Goodfellow is re-elected! Why, the national media will be camping on your doorstep!" (Tom Wetherly, whose doorstep was the one being discussed with such airy glibness, shuddered at this last comment, but he was a staunch and sturdy fellow, and of course he said nothing.)

"We do not wish to grace your pit-i-ful town coun-cil with our presence," Jarry muttered, but still Dewitt pressed onward. "Cooperate with us, Mr. Jarry," he promised, "and we'll give you your own office, in another building if you prefer. We'll make sure you get all the latest video cartridges. And," he added eagerly, leaning toward Jarry in a conspiratorial fashion, "you needn't attend council meetings if such things don't appeal to you. We are fully willing to be, uh, flexible in such matters."

Jarry stared at him with utter contempt. "You do not seem to com-pre-hend us," he said flatly. "We have no in-ter-est in the te-di-ous and tri-vi-al pas-times of mi-nor bu-reau-crats. Now we are grow-ing ve-ry bored. We are go-ing to go fish-ing." He rose from his chair, straightening out each limb one at a time like the blades on a jackknife, then marched out the door. Wetherly stayed behind just long enough to wish the flabber-gasted mayor and his apoplectic aide a quick farewell before dashing off after Jarry. He wasn't quite sure what had just happened, but he had a nagging suspicion that whatever it was, it was likely to have a few aftershocks.

When he saw the front page of the *Tribune*'s rival paper, the *Independent*, the next morning, he realized that he should have taken out some earthquake insurance. The *Independent*, which was actively endorsing Marshall Law, had gleefully described yesterday's meeting at City Hall as nothing short of a scandal! "Goodfellow Attempts To Seduce Pop Culture Figure in Last-Ditch Swing Vote Attempt!" sneered the triple-deck headline. As Wetherly scanned the article, he couldn't help but shudder when he encountered his own name a few graphs down. "Los Angeles *Tribune* reporter Thomas Wetherly, Jarry's public relations man,'" he groaned, inadvertently covering his eyes. This, he realized with a sinking heart, was not going to stand him in very good stead with his city editor at the Trib. He'd been missing far too much work lately as it was.

The *Independent*'s story was soon being discussed with great levity in bars and restaurants all over town. There was a considerable amount of jeering and less-than-charitable laughter, almost all of which was directed at the doubly hapless Mayor Goodfellow and especially at his overly zeal-ous campaign manager. At Marshall Law's campaign headquarters, the laughter was almost so robust as to be obscene. Law was in his glory: swaggering around, he promised that the minute he was elected he would run any and all weird foreign scum like this Jare-y fella right outta town on a rail. "Los Angeles for Americans!" he vowed, and his supporters cheered back at him, "We're gonna make this an American town again, by gosh!"

Soon to be ex-mayor Goodfellow's pronouncements were of a con-siderably less robust variety. The morning the story ran in the *Independent*, His Honor failed to show up for work at City Hall; it was only his third unexplained absence in his two terms of office. When Dana Dewitt called him at home to frame an apology, he discovered the reason for the mayor's absence: the generally temperate Goodfellow was suffering the aftereffects of a mammoth bender. "You're damn lucky I'm not going to have a third term, Dana," observed the mayor, his cracked, raw-sounding voice barely qualifying as a whisper.

"Why, Chief?" Dewitt wanted to know.

"BECAUSE IF I DID GET RE-ELECTED, I'D BE SURE YOU WERE THE FIRST JERK I FIRED!" Goodfellow suddenly shouted into the phone, turning the unsuspecting Dewitt's eardrum inside out.

But something even more unthinkable was about to transpire. A few days after the story of the City Hall meeting had hit the streets, the same blue-haired hooligans who loathed Mayor Goodfellow and adulated Jarry began showing up on Hollywood street corners to hand out crudely-drawn photocopied flyers. "Dump the fascist Law! Get rid of Goodfellow!" the flyers howled. "If we have to have a mayor, make him a man of the times! Write in Alfred Jarry on April 11!"

Jumping at the chance to save his admittedly waning honor, Wetherly quickly turned out another article for the *Tribune* about this ironic phenomenon. He pointed out that in a recent mayoral race in San Francisco, enough voters had written in the name of a punk rock singer, Jello Biafra, to have split the ticket, necessitating a runoff vote. "Perhaps the time has come for the voters to take the electoral process into their own hands," he said, ending his article on a tongue-in-cheek note.

Jarry himself exhibted his customary *noblesse oblige* and became an avid circuit rider in the week prior to the election, giving his version of campaign speeches in video arcades and laundromats. "If we are e-lec-ted to this ad-mit-ted-ly ri-dic-u-lous po-si-tion," he orated, "we will cause ab-sinthe to be sold in ev-er-y vid-e-o ar-cade." The crowds who turned out to hear him cheered loudly. Wetherly noticed that their numbers seemed to increase considerably every time Jarry made another appearance, but he still viewed the whole situation as a grotesque and exaggerated joke. Sure, the times were so rotten as to be downright laughable, but who could really take a fruitcake like Alfred Jarry seriously as a candidate?

Finally election day dawned, hot and sticky and sullen with smog. During his lunch break, Wetherly drove to his polling place, an elementary school in his neighborhood. In the voting booth he hesitated for a moment, his voting stylus poised above James C. Goodfellow's respectable-looking name. Then he grinned, whispered "What the fuck" under his breath, whipped out his ballpoint, and scrawled "Alfred Jarry" on the reverse side of the ballot in the write-in section. When he handed his ballot to the elderly lady sitting beside the ballot box, he realized that he was feeling better than he could remember having felt in years. Not that Al was likely to win, of course; there wasn't a chance in hell of that. But the sheer irrationality of the act of bypassing the two accepted, conventional choices on the ballot in favor of a total madman was, Wetherly had to admit, incredibly heady. Maybe this was the key to Alfred's seemingly inexplicable popularity, he thought—the way Alfred somehow managed to convey the excitement of committing a purely irrational act for no other reason than because it was irrational. As he drove back to the Trib, Wetherly found himself remembering a statement of Alfred's that had gotten lodged in his mind, and which, like many of Jarry's quotable quotes, almost made sense if you said it fast enough: "Be-yond left and right there is one di-rec-tion—a-bove." It seemed to sum up the tone of this particular election, anyway.

Twelve hours later the ballots were all in, the votes were all counted, and Alfred Jarry was discovered to be the first write-in candidate ever elected mayor of Los Angeles. Because the margins were amazingly close, both Law and Goodfellow immediately demanded a recount. It was taken, but the original total was found to be accurate. Then Goodfellow conceded defeat, but Law doggedly insisted on a runoff between himself and Jarry. "I smell something fishy here!" he whined. "This scummy dwarf isn't even an American! I'll bet he's a commonist spy!"

Due consultation of the proper documents by the appropriate officers revealed that there was no call for a runoff; even though there was no precedent for it, Jarry's candidacy had been insisted upon by the voting public. He had won the seat fair and square. There was nothing left but to swear him in.

Jarry's first act as mayor of Los Angeles was to call a press conference—an idea given him by Tom Wetherly, who had suddenly found himself serving as full-time muncipal errand runner, city hall press agent, and deputy mayor (during Jarry's absinthe). The idea of calling a press conference may have been Wetherly's, but the decision to hold it in a large and extremely seedy video arcade on Hollywood Boulevard was strictly His Honor's. Wetherly knew better than to try to dissuade him, so on the appointed date, a week after Jarry's election, all the electronic and print journalists in town began converging on the spot in question—a very questionable spot indeed. From the very beginning, the event promised to be royally entertaining. Long, imposing mobile video units hove into sight and vied for a severely limited number of parking spaces, and well-dressed journalists with apprehensive expressions came sidling down Hollywood Boulevard in dubious twos and threes, peering nervously behind every corner for potential thugs. Things were off to a great start.

At exactly 2:00 p.m. LAPT (Los Angeles Pataphysical Time, which Jarry had declared to be the new standard measurement), flashbulbs began popping and minicams started whirring furiously as the new mayor came striding slowly and majestically toward a podium which had been placed near the flyblown snack bar. Resplendent in a pair of women's deep purple nylon-and-rubber sweat pants and a black tuxedo jacket which had undoubtedly been quite handsome twenty years earlier, His Honor marched up to the podium, where he climbed onto a pile of telephone directories placed strategically behind it (intended to elevate his diminutive person to a visible height).

For the next hour he addressed himself to many topics: the political situation in Lichtenstein, Ozzy Osbourne, terminal illnesses, motor scooters, Nora Ephron, postcard collectors . . . When Wetherly finally prodded him to open the floor to questions from the press, a dozen annoyed voices rang out at once with numerous variations on the basic theme of ''What the hell are you trying to pull, anyway?'' But Jarry remained as unruffled as the stagnant surface of a dead marsh. ''We do not like your ques-tions at all,'' he observed airily. ''They are too spe-ci-fic and bor-ing. In sci-ence we do not at-tempt to con-fine our spec-u-la-tions to one lit-tle cor-ner of thought, but ra-ther to broad-en our per-son-al cor-ner of thought with the end-less spec-trum of u-ni-ver-sal pos-si-bi-li-ties.''

''Your Honor,'' shouted a red-faced reporter from the rear of the room, shaking his notebook at Jarry with considerable impatience, ''the public has a right to know what your policies are going to be! You're an elected official, duly sworn to serve the citizens of Los Angeles! Just what are Pataphysics, anyway?'' he added. This turned out to be an extremely grave mistake, for it caused His Honor to embark upon another long-winded spiel that no one could even begin to comprehend. The moment His Honor paused to catch his breath and to take a gulp from a bottled mixture of green Chartreuse and Yoo-Hoo chocolate soda stationed strategically inside the podium, Tom Wetherly moved quickly forward and began to shoo the bewildered and rebellious media out of the arcade. ''If you have any further questions you can contact me at City Hall this afternoon,'' he pleaded in what he hoped was a firm and authoritative tone.

When the last irate newsperson had finally been sent packing, the thoroughly exhausted Wetherly sought out the mayor. He found Jarry in front of a video machine, manipulating a long, slippery joystick with grim relish as the game emitted a series of tinny electronic groans and gasps. ''We are a-bout to reach a pla-teau,'' he announced as he spotted Wetherly approaching.

''Al,'' Tom began wearily, slumping onto the slippery formica top of the machine next to Jarry's, ''there are a few things you ought to know about holding public office.''

"What we do not know al-rea-dy, we are not in-ter-es-ted in know-ing," snapped Jarry. "And right now we in-fin-ite-ly pre-fer man-ip-u-la-ting this plas-tic phal-lus to en-dur-ing your mo-no-to-nous spee-ches."

Tom shook his head. "All right, Al," he said wearily. "Have it your way for the time being, but remember, the public is paying your salary, and if they decide they don't like you, they can 86 you so fast your head'll spin—pataphysics or no pataphysics."

"We have ta-ken the pre-cau-tion of draw-ing our first month's sa-la-ry and hav-ing it con-ver-ted into quar-ters," observed His Honor, gestur-ing toward an oversized shoebox lying on the floor at his feet. Wetherly glanced down with mingled amusement and horror and saw that it was filled to overflowing with silver coins. Shaking his head, he bid Jarry farewell and was heading out the door when the mayor called after him, "On your way to the pa-lace of jus-tice you can stop and pick up some more dried peas for our pea-shoo-ter."

When Wetherly arrived at City Hall a little later that afternoon, an economy-size bag of dried peas tucked dutifully under his arm, he was im-mediately accosted by Jarry's executive secretary, Mrs. Tintype. It was not a pretty sight: something had reduced the ordinarily handsome, effi-cient, and reliable Mrs. Tintype to a twisted and palpitating bundle of jangled nerves. In fact, the underlying current of her stoically suppressed agony seemed almost violent enough to cause a rent in her guaranteed-indestructable polyester pants. "Mr. Wetherly, I'm so glad you're here," she gasped, flinging herself into the chair behind her desk and gathering into her arms an enormous sheaf of telephone messages. "Lori is out sick today, so I've been handling all the mayor's incoming calls. I haven't had one minute to do anything else beside answer the phone."

Stricken mute with astonishment, Wetherly took the awe-inspiring stack of messages from Mrs. Tintype's nerveless arms. Many were from national TV news programs, requesting interviews with the mayor ASAP. One was from the editor-in-chief, no less, of *Time* magazine, requesting an exclusive interview; a little further down the pile Wetherly found a duplicate request from the editor-in-chief of *Newsweek*. Apparently the news of Jarry's press conference had traveled fast. As Wetherly stood in a shock-induced stupor, trying with futility to comprehend the gravity of the situation, the phone rang again. He awoke partially from his sub-consciousness to find Mrs. Tintype tugging catatonically at his sleeve.

"Mr. Wetherly? It's the news director of the '50/50' program in New York. They'd like to interview the mayor there as soon as possible."

"My God," mumbled Wetherly, picking up the phone, "I always knew Al loved being in the public eye, but I never dreamed that one day he might become a real live media sleazeball."

The next Sunday afternoon, Tom and Mary Ann Utterly huddled in front of the TV in Wetherly's apartment, nervously anticipating Mayor Jarry's first national television appearance. So many different programs had clamored for His Honor that he had gone off to New York to make the most of the media blitz. (Tom had spent an interminable night wrestling with his conscience before finally reaching the conclusion that New York could probably defend itself against Jarry, provided it was given a fighting chance.) In Alfred's absence, Mary Ann was staying at Tom's, an arrangement which ordinarily would have delighted Wetherly if he hadn't had his hands so full of other, far less enjoyable, activities around City Hall. Having asked for and grudgingly received an indefinite leave of absence from the *Tribune*, he was devoting himself to the deputy mayorship—primarily to cleaning up after the mayor, whose personal style of disengagement was rapidly becoming legendary.

Thinking about the magnitude of his responsibilities until such time as Jarry might be impeached, Tom sighed and put his arm around Mary Ann's round, smooth back. As he fiddled affectionately with her bra strap under her T-shirt, he idly wondered if His Most Arbitrary Honor had turned the entire city fiscal budget into quarters, or if he, Wetherly, might be able to ask for an advance on his pay and receive a relatively unpataphysical answer.

"Sshhh," cautioned Mary Ann needlessly as a very wide smile appeared on the small screen, filling it nearly to the corners. "Good evening, wadies and gentlemen," said a disembodied female voice. "Tonight we are going to be talking to Awfred Jawy, mayor of Woss Angewess, Cawifownia. As you may awready know, Mr. Jawy has been in the news a gweat deal lately because of his wather unique pewsonal and powitical style. Wewcome to New Yock, Your Honow." The camera pulled back to reveal a large, high-ceilinged room whose chief feature was a maroon quasi-Victorian sofa. Slumping sullenly in its exact center was Jarry, scowling at a blonde women seated in a pseudo-Edwardian armchair across from him. Closer inspection revealed that she was the owner/ operator of the big smile and the disembodied voice.

"Somewhere in Manhattan, a clotheshorse with a cleft palate is grilling a pint-sized nihilist," Tom grumbled sarcastically.

"Ssshhh," repeated Mary Ann, caressing his cheek with her long, cool fingers. Tom leaned back restively, wondering just how Jarry was going to conduct himself. He knew that trouble was inevitable; it always was with Jarry. The exhausting and entertaining part was not anticipating the trouble itself, but trying to second-guess the precise nature of the diabolical dwarf's crazed activities before Jarry could wreak too much havoc on the unsuspecting, the guileless, and the innocent.

"Your Honow," began the woman on the screen, buttressing every word with another burst of the smile, "befowe we go any fuwther, I want to bwing up a vewy intewesting fact that I wan across the other day. I happened to be weading a biogwaphy of a turn-of-the-centuwy Pawisian litewawy figure whose name was, cuwiously enough, awso Awfred Jawy." (A line of type flashed across the screen: "*Alfred Jarry: The Man with the Axe*, by Nigey Lennon with illustrations by Bill Griffith, Panjandrum Books, Los Angeles.") "This Awfred Jawy was the authow of a scandalous play called *Ubu Woi*, which was appawently so vulgar and howible that it weaked weal hovoc in Pawis when it pwemiewed in 1896. But what I found especially intewesting was the fact that this Awfred Jawy had a vewy outwageous lifestyle, chawactewized by bizaw and thowoughly inappwopwiate behaviow—very much, in fact, like your own.

"Now level with us, Your Honow. You've been quoted as saying that you were yourself an authow in Pawis at the turn of the centuwy. You do things like holding pwess confewences in video arcades and bouncing dwied peas off the heads of city council members duwing council meetings. Tell us, Your Honow—who are you *weally*, and where are you weally fwom?" The blond woman leaned forward expectantly into Jarry's face, which had been growing increasingly darker throughout this surprising revelation. Tom suddenly slapped his thigh. "That's it!" he exclaimed. "I knew I'd stumbled across it all somewhere before!"

"Sssssshhhhh," hissed Mary Ann. "Alfred is going to answer her."

Up on the screen, Jarry did seem about to respond. With his thick, inky brows knit together in manic concentration on his deeply-creased forehead, he protruded stiffly from the edge of the sofa like a gargoyle on a cornice. There was no denying the phosphorescent murder radiating from the depths of his bottomless black eyes. Tom, sensing impending doom, bore down on the arm of the couch until all his knuckles cracked. "I hope they're on a six-second delay," he babbled irrelevantly.

As Mary Ann and Tom strained closer to the TV, the metallic, disembodied sound of Jarry's voice came spewing out of the speaker. Tom had to fight off a persistent illusion that the TV itself, rather than Jarry, was somehow speaking. "Ma-dame, we do not doubt that any mat-ter more com-plex than the se-lec-tion of bou-doir fi-ne-ry or the va-ga-ries of some re-ci-pe or oth-er is far be-yond your a-bi-li-ties of com-pre-hen-sion," snarled the TV. Then Jarry suddenly leaped up off the sofa, an overwound clock snapping its mainspring. "We do not wish to con-tin-ue this i-di-o-tic con-ver-sa-tion," he growled over his shoulder as he went staggering away off-camera. For a brief, chaotic moment, there was a lingering and obviously unintentional shot of the interviewer's face, her mouth flapping like a landed trout's, her eyes threatening to explode out of their sockets, and her complexion a most unbecoming mottle of furious technicolor splotches. Then, just as the audio began to fade into the program's light, bubbly theme music, her last comment came blasting out over the airwaves into countless millions of homes: "That nasty little fwaud! He just bit me in the fucking ankle!"

Ludicrously, a commercial for floor wax flitted hesitantly across the screen, then complete and immutable darkness closed down. The chaos had reached its ultimate conclusion.

Jarry had been scheduled to return to Los Angeles following an appearance on "Late Night with David Letterman," but the day of his ostensible homecoming came and went without any sign of him. Wetherly, filled with doubts and forebodings, put through an anxious call to the producer of the "Letterman" show, only to be told that Jarry had never showed up at the studio to tape his segment of the program, nor had he sent any message or excuse explaining his failure to appear. Jarry seemed simply to have vanished as precipitously as he had originally appeared.

After hanging up, Tom poured himself a Jack Daniel's and settled back into a watery morass of rumination. Manhattan may have survived everything from the 1929 Wall Street crash to the tumultuous arrival of the Beatles at the Plaza Hotel in 1964, but he still doubted whether it had any chance whatsoever when it came to Alfred Jarry. As he sat there drunkenly, a paranoid panorama of scenes went parading across the screen of his mind. He visualized Jarry terrorizing even the hardest-boiled of cabbies with unfathomably pataphysical destinations. He shuddered as he imagined his demonic roommate suddenly appearing in some over-priced restaurant and ordering a seven-course dinner in his usual fashion —inside-out, starting with dessert and ending with soup. And he even pitied the haughty and high-handed waiter who might dare to challenge Jarry's culinary peccadilloes, being blissfully unaware that the little tyrant never went anywhere without both pistols fully loaded.

No, the scenario was not exactly a pleasant one. But the worst part of it was that Tom found himself actually missing Alfred. Jarry's behavior had always been singularly erratic and unpredictable, but whatever his adventures out in the world, he had brought an intense interest into Tom's life. Suddenly, the thought of life without Jarry seemed flat, dull, mundane. Tom wondered if he could ever get worked up over cable TV or weekend trips to Mammoth again.

By the time the bottle of Jack Daniel's was half empty, he was sniffing sentimentally and making dangerous promises: "If old Al would just show up on the doorstep, I'd never yell at him again for writing all night. Hell, I wouldn't even holler if he stuck a dead mackerel down the pants to my best suit and left it there for a month."

But Jarry did not reappear. The days turned into weeks without a word from him, and Wetherly found himself heavy-heartedly adopting the duties of mayor *pro tem*. It did not take him long to realize that he was totally unfit for the position. Compared to his predecessor, he was sadly deficient when it came to catching fish in the Los Angeles River or pre-cipitately ending City Council meetings with a few cannily chosen, in-comprehensible sentences.

As the weeks passed, Tom became resigned to his loss, although never thoroughly accepting of it. Nonetheless, Wetherly was careful never to look in the closet where Alfred's bicycle still reposed. He knew that his heart wouldn't be able to stand the strain.

Then one day the mail brought the news that Wetherly had been so desperate for. Along with the usual bills and junk mail, Tom instantly spotted a smeary envelope bearing Jarry's oddly literate penmanship. It was postmarked Vincennes, Indiana, and was addressed simply to "M. Tom Whether-or-not, Les Anges, Californie." Wetherly had no idea how it had reached him; he assumed that Jarry had not yet succeeded in pataphysicizing the postal service.

With hands that trembled almost uncontrollably, he ripped open the envelope. Inside was a single sheet of lined notebook paper, spotted with ample evidence of alcoholic dissipation. His heart began to pound as he scanned the erratic but graceful lines that sprawled uphill on the grimy page. "We are, as they say, getting down with our bad self. We merely grew tired of our position in that tiresome swamp of a bourgeois city council, and (yes, we admit it!) became homesick for the illuminating taste of absinthe and for the sight of the corpses that float sometimes at midnight in the Seine. Perhaps we will even press on to Turkistan in our search for bigger fish to catch. Please be good enough to look after that which rolls"—this was his term for his bicycle, of course—"as well as our—"

There was a break in the writing here, and a huge black blot (Jarry was obviously writing with a quill dipped in a mixture comprised at least partially of India ink), then an alcohol stain which rendered the next couple of lines illegible. By puzzling over the remainder of the note for more than an hour, Tom was finally able to decipher its closing line: "Remind that woman that her place is not in the kitchen, as we would prefer to reserve that station for ourself. We remain pataphysically yours, A.-H. Jarry."

Wetherly reread this curious epistle perhaps fifteen times. Case-hardened cynic that he was, he still couldn't prevent a few drops of moisture from welling up in his eyes and flowing, unchecked, down the curve of his cheek. "Damn you, Al," he muttered, "damn you. But I hope where you're going there's plenty of absinthe to guzzle, that the fish never stop biting, and that you never run out of quarters."

Then, gazing at the TV set across the room, he added in a choked voice: "And if you ever get tired of wandering, remember that L.A.'s your town, you little maniac."

BIBLIOGRAPHY

PRIMARY SOURCES

Chauveau, Paul. *Alfred Jarry ou la naissance, la vie et la mort du Père Ubu*. Paris: Le Mercure de France, 1932.

Cooper, Judith. *Ubu Roi: An Analytical Study*. Tulane University, New Orleans, Louisiana: Tulane Studies in Romance Languages and Literature, November 6, 1974.

Esslin, Martin. *The Theater of the Absurd*. Garden City, New York: Anchor Books, Doubleday and Company, Inc., 1961.

LaBelle, Maurice M. *Alfred Jarry: Nihilism and the Theater of the Absurd*. New York and London: New York University Press, 1980.

Levesque, Jacques-Henry. *Alfred Jarry ("Poètes d'Aujord'hui"* No. 24. Paris: Editions Pierre Seghers, 1967.)

Lot, Fernand. *Alfred Jarry, son oeuvre, portrait et autographe*. Paris: Editions de la Nouvelle Revue Critique, 1934.

Perche, Louis. *Alfred Jarry ("Classiques du XXe Siecle."* Paris: Editions Universitaires, 1965.)

Rachilde (Marguerite Eymery Vallette). *Alfred Jarry ou le surmâle de lettres. ("La Vie de Boheme."* Paris: Bernard Grasset, 1928.)

Shattuck, Roger. *The Banquet Years: The Origins of the Avant-Garde, 1885 To World War I*. New York: Vintage Books/Random House, 1968 (revised edition).

Roger Shattuck's essay, "What Is 'Pataphysics?," along with a number of brief articles by other writers about some of Jarry's contemporaries, appear in *The Evergreen Review Reader, Vol. I, 1957-1961* (New York: Grove Press, 1979.)

WORKS BY ALFRED JARRY AVAILABLE IN ENGLISH TRANSLATIONS

Selected Works of Alfred Jarry. Roger Shattuck and Simon Watson Taylor, translators. New York: Grove Press, 1965.

The Ubu Plays. Cyril Connolly and Simon Watson Taylor, translators. New York: Grove Press, 1969.

Ubu Roi. Barbara Wright, translator. New York: New Directions, 1961.

King Turd (translations of the Ubu plays). Beverley Keith and G. Legman, translators. New York: Boar's Head Books, 1953.

Caesar-Antichrist (play). James H. Bierman, translator. Tucson, Arizona: Omen Press, 1971.

The Supermale (Le surmâle) (novel). Ralph Gladstone and Barbara Wright, translators. New York: New Directions, 1964.

MISCELLANEOUS NOTES

Research Sources, The Collège de 'Pataphysique, and Various Frustrations. In writing this biography I made liberal use of the materials in the French Literature and Drama sections of the library at California State University, Long Beach. During my research, the assistance of that library's head of Special Collections, Mr. John Ahouse, proved indispensable. I also conducted research at the University of California, Los Angeles research library, and at the Central Library in downtown Los Angeles. A number of private individuals lent me rare Jarry materials, including my charming and generous publisher, Dennis Koran.

The chief repository of Jarryana in the known world is the Collège de 'Pataphysique, which was founded in Paris in 1949. Over the years this organization has published numerous special publications and books on Jarry's life and work, including the *Cahiers* and *Dossiers* (Notebooks and Files, respectively). However, it has proved virtually impossible to deal with the Collège by mail from the United States. They simply do not respond to letters, whether due to understaffing or perhaps because they consider letters requesting specific information to be unpataphysical by nature. Furthermore, official Regents of the Collège de 'Pataphysique based in the United States have been equally unwilling to answer letters from myself and my publisher regarding translations of Jarry's writing. I guess professional pataphysicians are just a gang of rugged individualists.

A Note on Translations: In the original French, there are two Jarry *Oeuvres completes*—a 1948 collection, published in Monte Carlo and Lausanne, which is notorious for its numerous inaccuracies and omissions; and a 1974 collection published by Gallimard in Paris. In English translation the selection is considerably more spotty, with the quality of the translations varying from inspired to inexcusable. There are a number of difficulties facing the would-be Jarry translator; the primary one being Jarry's habitual use of deliberately ambiguous words and phrases, which are totally impossible to render in English without "concretizing" them and thus obliterating their subtlety. Another problem lies in trying to find acceptable substitutes for many of the words in Jarry's brilliant but perverse idioglossia, which indiscriminately mingles schoolboy slang, "medieval" French, Latin scientific terms, and various disjointed and displaced literary words and phrases collected by Jarry during a brief but intense lifetime of reading.

Of the existing translations, as an introduction to Jarry's writing style I would recommend Ralph Gladstone and Barbara Wright's translation of *The Supermale* and (if you can find it) a 1902 article Jarry wrote for the *Revue Blanche* entitled "Barnum," which appears in translation by Peter Wood in the book *Surrealism and Its Popular Accomplices* (Franklin Rosemont, editor; San Francisco: City Lights Books, 1980). And of course, *The Selected Works of Alfred Jarry* is, by virtue of merely existing, crucial to any Jarry fiend's library. Meanwhile, despite the assorted obstacles that confront the Jarry translator, it is fervently hoped that there will eventually be a "Complete Works" in English, and that we won't have to wait until the bicentennial of Jarry's birth (2073) for this most grievous literary lack to be remedied.

INDEX

127

Offset printed in Trump Medieval
with Clearface Black chapter titles,
the book was typeset by sending data,
without rekeying, from the author's
Radio Shack TRS 80 directly to the
typesetter's Kaypro II. From there the
data was sent to the CompuGraphic MCS
at Freedmen's Organization in Los
Angeles, where it was paginated and
output on the 8400 digital typesetter.